MANNERS AND MORALS of VICTORIAN AMERICA

by WAYNE ERBSEN

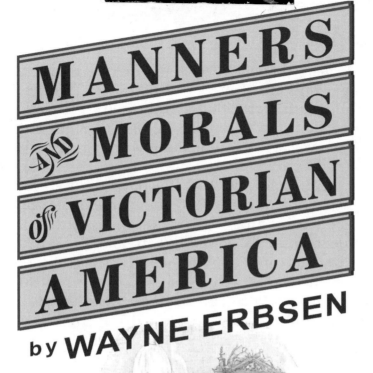

Native Ground Books & Music, Asheville, North Carolina

Credits

I would only be good manners to thank all the people who contributed to this book. Thanks to Barbara Swell, John Miller, and Kelli Churchill for inspiration and perspiration, and to Steve Millard for the cover art. Thanks, gang, for putting up with me.

In a strange way, this book really started four years ago. On a quest to find some long out-of-print books, I got several lucky breaks and managed to connect with Susan Duncan, whose late husband, John Duncan, had written a number of books under the pseudonym of Sam Tuttle. In talking with Susan, I discovered that Sam had once written a book called *Manners & Morals of Yesterday*. Although John long had passed on, the basement of the home he shared with his wife was still filled with hundreds of boxes of this book. I bought all of them.

When we finally sold the last of Sam's books, I decided against reprinting it. As interesting as the book was, I found it to be somewhat frustrating because Sam neglected to cite his sources. As an historian, I needed to know the what, the where, and the when. In this new book you are holding, I fixed this problem in *spades*. Practically ever single quote is referenced by a date which corresponds to the books listed in chronological order in the bibliography. Besides giving you the sources of the quotes, I've also dated the nearly 500 illustrations that adorn this book. A piece of art which is lacking a date usually means it came from Sam Tuttle's original book. In the interest of saving space, I have only provided the date, not the exact source, of the art.

I must tell you that I had the most fun researching this book. If you have half the fun reading as I did putting it together, you're in for a very good time.

July 2014   ISBN 978-1-883206-54-3

NGB-959

Library of Congress Control Number: 2008943591

1882

Contents

Contents

PREFACE

"Manners make the man."

THE first time I mentioned to my family and friends that I was writing a book on 19th century manners and etiquette, there was a moment of total silence followed by blank stares and several snickers. "What's so funny about that?" I innocently asked, knowing full well that I have never been known for having picture perfect manners. In fact, the shocking fact is that my own personal manners are somewhat "relaxed." Some might leave off the first part of that word and simply call them "lax."

I soon reminded these naysayers that my new book isn't about me trying to inflict my personal manners on an unsuspecting public. Heaven forbid! Instead, wearing the hat of a professional historian, I literally pawed through thousands of pages of 19th century and early 20th century etiquette manuals to extract gems of both wisdom and folly. The material I included is somewhat light on manners such as how to hold your fork, but heavy on looking at how Victorians adapted to newfangled inventions like the bicycle, the telephone, the phonograph, and the motor-car. As you go through the book, you'll see how Victorians adjusted to the social and economic forces that were changing the face of America. Young couples were warned against the dangers of "spooning," parents were taught the benefits of chaperones for their daughters, gentlemen were instructed to doff their hats and how to hand a lady in or out of a carriage. Ladies were shown how to crank their new motor-car without breaking an arm.

SEARS MOTOR BUGGY $395

Preface

As many Americans in the late 19th century moved to the bustling cities, they took jobs and started businesses that helped them become more prosperous. Along with their growing wealth, there was a national obsession with looking and acting the part. Hundreds of etiquette and manners books literally flooded the market and were gobbled up by a public yearning to be accepted by the "upper crust" or "old money" families. It is from these books that I've selected choice quotes that spotlight both fascinating similarities and differences to our own times.

1903

Lucky for us, the avalanche of these turn-of-the century etiquette books coincided with the golden age of Victorian art. Many of the books I discovered were profusely illustrated, so I had a virtual gold mine of incredible art at my fingertips. That helped to make this as much a picture book as a word book.

To give you the full flavor of 19th and early 20th century speech and thought, I've done little or no editing of the writing of the Victorian era authors I've quoted. At the end of each quote you'll find the date it was first published. Beyond putting the quote in its historical context, these dates also serve as footnotes and correlate with the bibliography on pages 178-179.

So tuck in your shirt, sit up straight, take off your hat and pretend you have manners. Now you're ready for your first lesson in Victorian etiquette. Please turn the page.

Clogs & Fetters

MANY a man would give much to be rid of habits fastened upon him in youth, and which have been clogs and fetters, making every step of progress in certain directions toilsome and painful. He has accomplished only half of what he might have accomplished but for these annoying and irritating shackles. (1889c)

Misery on a Train

In a railway coach, it is a distinct misery to sit near a party of people who are eating peanuts and scattering shells upon the floor, and the odor of oranges and bananas on a train is nauseating. (1910)

Annoying Children

Never allow a child to pull a visitor's dress, play with the jewelry or ornaments she may wear, take her parasol or satchel for a plaything, or in any way annoy her. (1910)

Whispering

Do not read the newspaper in an audible whisper, as it disturbs the attention of these near you. Remember, that a carelessness as to what may incommode others is the sure sign of a coarse and ordinary mind. (1860)

1897

Nail Biting

Biting the nails is one of the most annoying habits, and yet one which almost any boy will fall into unless his mother "nips it in the bud." A habit of tapping the floor with the foot, or the table with the knuckles, comes on gradually, but, once fixed, is exceedingly difficult to overcome. "Eternal vigilance" should be a mother's watchword, for the true secret of curing bad habits is in never allowing them to be formed. The "ounce of prevention" is worth more than the "pound of cure." (*Manford's Magazine*, 1885)

1891

Fidgetiness in Public

Avoid restlessness in company, lest you make the whole party as fidgety as yourself. (1860)

Calling with Children and Pets

Callers should never take children or pets with them, as they are apt to be very annoying to some people. (1889b)

The Devil's Tattoo

Do not beat "the devil's tattoo" by drumming with your fingers on a table; it cannot fail to annoy every one within hearing, and it is an index of a vacant mind. (1843)

1889

Beating Time

F you are at a concert, or a private musical party, do not beat time with your feet or a cane upon the floor. It is mighty vexatious. It is not fashionable to applaud at the play, for doing so might indicate a natural emotion, and every thing like feeling is now out of fashion. A gentleman, and man of sense, however, will applaud, and that heartily. (1836)

Civility at Concerts

It is rude to whisper or talk during a performance. It is discourteous to the performers, and annoying to those of the audience around you, who desire to enjoy the entertainment. To seek to draw attention to yourself at a place of amusement is simply vulgar. (1896b)

Two young ladies were once singing a duet in a concert-room. A stranger who had heard better performances, turned to his neighbor saying, "Does not the young lady in white sing wretchedly?" "Excuse me sir," replied he, "I scarcely feel at liberty to express my sentiments; she is my sister." "I beg your pardon, sir," he answered, "I mean the lady in blue." " You are perfectly right there," replied the neighbor, "I have often told her so myself; she is my wife."

(Frank Leslie's Pleasant Hours, 1878)

Attending Concerts

Manners at Concerts

We should observe the most profound silence, and refrain from beating time, humming the airs, applauding, or making ridiculous gestures of admiration. (1841)

Applause

Applause is the just due of the deserving actor, and should be given liberally. Applaud by clapping the hands, and not by stamping or kicking with the feet. (1896b)

Attending with a Lady

In accompanying women to any public place, as to a concert, you should precede them in entering the room, and procure seats for them. (1836)

Conduct for a Gentleman

On entering the hall, theater or opera house the gentleman should walk side by side with his companion unless the aisle is too narrow, in which case he should precede her. Upon reaching the seats, he should allow her to take the inner one, assuming the outer one himself. (1882)

1883

The Gentle Art of Cycling

1896

CYCLING has found its legitimate place at last; it is as the gentle art. Women and elderly men have done much to raise cycling to the Gentle Art. It is a companion to the solitary, a friend that is always exhilarating and never selfish, an aid to reflection; it gives inspiration to the poet, health and strength to the plain man, vigour to the man of science, and breadth to the philosopher. (*Macmillan's Magazine*, 1898)

Driving Our Youth Crazy

To be held down to a snail's progress of four miles an hour by steady toe-and-heel tramping, and then suddenly to be gifted with the power of flying through the air at the rate of fourteen miles an hour with no more exertion than that entailed in walking — this was intoxication that at one time promised to send our youth crazy. (*Macmillan's Magazine*, 1898)

Objectionable Intimacies

1880

A marked feature of social life, is the introduction of the bicycle. No woman of good sense will practice scorching [speeding]. Neither will she offend the law by riding on the sidewalk, or donning an immodest costume, or make new acquaintances while on her wheel. One becomes intoxicated with delight at the swift rush in the open, and forgets convention. Objectionable intimacies have been formed between riders whose acquaintance began in the street. (*Good Housekeeping*, 1898)

Bicycling With a Lady

A man bicycling with a woman should extend to her all the courtesies practiced when riding or driving with her, such as allowing her to set the pace, taking the lead on unfamiliar roads and in dangerous places, riding on the side nearest obstacles, etc. (1904)

Convincing Her to Ride

No matter how adverse to wheeling a woman may be, if by any means she can be coaxed to the front seat of a tandem and given a spin over a good road, her conversion is a forgone conclusion. (*The Ladies' World*, June, 1897)

The Stronger Sex

The ordinary woman is at a great disadvantage in riding long distances with her husband or escort, when both are mounted upon single wheels. Man is the stronger sex, and will continue to be for some time, let us hope, so why, if he can, should he not give of his strength for the comfort of his weaker companion, even in the matter of cycling? (*The Ladies' World*, June, 1897)

Out of Style

The bicycle is not now quite as fashionable as it was a few years ago, particularly in cities. (1910)

The Cycle of the Future
THE "RIPEST FRUIT OF INVENTION"

1897

The Bow

HE bow is the touchstone of good breeding. It is a civility to return a bow although you do not know the one who is bowing to you. Bowing once to a person on a public promenade is all that civility requires. (1910)

Etiquette of the Horse-Car

For Ladies — Never accept a seat from a gentleman without acknowledging the courtesy by a bow and an audible expression of thanks. (1889)

1905

The Dance Bow

A gentleman should always make a bow to a lady when asking her to dance, and both of them should bow and say "Thank you" when the dance is over. (1887)

The Curtsey vs. the Bow

Formerly it was the habit for the ladies to curtsey on being introduced, but this has been changed into the more easy and graceful custom of bowing. (1868)

The Ideal Business Man

OVERCOMES obstacles to success, by *perseverance*.

- Protects himself from the moral leprosy of idleness by cultivating habits of judicious *industry*.
- Prevents confusion by thoughtful *arrangement*.
- Saves precious time by *punctuality*.
- Shuns snares and pitfalls by *prudence*.
- Avoids cheating any man of his due of courtesy and consideration by *tact*.
- Adjusts his expenditure to his income by *calculation*.
- Secures respect and confidence by his *truthfulness*.

The ideal business man is honorable, upright, and just, a man of principle rather than expediency. (1889)

Only Work and No Play

We Americans are too grave a people; we laugh too little; we amuse ourselves too little; we make business the "be-all and the end-all" of life. Work is both better done, and more thoroughly done, when varied and intermingled with recreation. (1868)

Never, Never

- Never fail to settle all debts promptly.
- Never buy on credit, if cash can be had.
- Never keep washer-women, seamstresses, nor anyone dependent upon daily labor waiting for payment.
- Never adopt a disagreeable manner when requesting payment of a debt.
- Never shirk labor, nor fail to devote the whole attention to the work in hand. (1889)

Laying Aside the Bonnet

1877

WING to the difficulty of rearranging most modern headgear of women, ladies are not expected to remove their bonnets when making a brief call. (1889b)

Hat in Hand

Keep your hat in your hand when making a call. This will show your host that you do not intend to remain to dine or sup with him. In making an evening call for the first time, keep your hat and gloves in your hand until the host or hostess requests you to lay them aside and spend the evening. (1875)

Waiting in the Parlor

While waiting in the parlor for the person on whom you have called, do not thump on an open piano, nor walk about the room examining pictures and other articles. (1889b)

Calling Upon a Person at Lodgings

When calling upon a person who has lodgings at a hotel or private house, remain below and send up your card. (1889b)

Looking at Your Watch

It is in bad taste for a caller to preface his or her departure by consulting a watch, remarking, "Now I must go," or insinuating that the hostess is weary of the visitor. (1869)

The Chaperone

HAPERONES are usually of one of three ages — marriage, parentage, or dotage. Their charges are universally of one age — bondage. (1906b)

Protector of Young Women

Our cosmopolitan cities are thronged with strangers. Our streets are crowded. The chaperone has now become an important figure in society. She accompanies the girl to the place of public amusement. She attends her at the social function in a private house. She goes driving with her in the park, and if the girl is quite young, she is not permitted to shop or to call unless she has the older woman with her. (1910)

Duties of the Chaperone

The chaperone is the Good Shepherd of the flock. She must ceaselessly lead her lambs into the green pastures and beside the still waters of the social swim. (1906b)

1877

Old Eagle-Eye

The ever-vigilante chaperons are to keep an eagle-eye on the young girls in their care to prevent them from committing indiscretions at a debutante's ball. (1910)

Three's a Crowd

There is but one motto: "Two's company and three's a crowd!" It is forever up to the chaperone to syndicate the two-some and make it "a crowd." (1906b)

Manners for Tots

HE tiny child must be taught to remove his hat when he is spoken to, to give his hand readily in greeting, to say "please" and "thank you;" not to pass in front of people, or between them and the fire; to say "excuse me" when he trods on his mother's foot or dress; to rise when she enters the room; and to take off his hat when he kisses her. (1905)

Never Too Early

We cannot too early begin to teach children how to behave. As soon as a babe is in this world, its education must begin. (1910)

THE GREATEST WOMAN IN THE WORLD—"MA"

1912

"I Don't Care If I Do"

A little boy was asked by his uncle if he wanted some flowers, and replied, "I don't care if I do." The uncle said, "I never give flowers to boys who don't care." Whereupon the urchin responded: "I don't care if I do, but I do care if I don't."

(*Frank Leslie's Pleasant Hours,* 1885)

Pesky Children

Never allow a child to play with a visitor's hat or cane. (1910)

Do not leave children to their own devices near a lion's cage. (1910)

Children and Dogs

Some people prefer children to dogs, principally because a licence is not required for the former. (1910b)

Forgo the Curls

The mother should strive to make her boy look manly. Possibly as a pet, her boy has in infancy had his hair curled. Even now, when he is six or eight years of age, the curls look very pretty. But the mother must forgo her further pleasure in the curls; for the boy, to take his place along with the others, to run and jump, to grow manly and strong, must wear short hair. His mother can no longer dress it like a girl's. It will be necessary and best to cut off the curls. (1910)

1903

Beware of Bad Books

One-half of the youth in our prisons and houses of correction started on their evil careers by reading bad books, or at best, worthless novels. These books are the nicotine and alcohol of literature; they poison and burn, and blast the head and heart as surely as their cousins do the stomach. (1916)

1870

Forbearance With Children

A guest should not notice nor find fault with the bad behavior of the children in the household where visiting, and should put up with any of their faults, and overlook any ill-bred or disagreeable actions on their part. (1882)

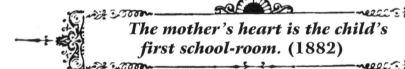

The mother's heart is the child's first school-room. (1882)

Children and Visitors

Do not allow your children to be troublesome to visitors; to climb upon them, soil their dresses with their fingers, handle their jewelry and ornaments, ask annoying questions, nor intrude themselves into their private apartments at unseasonable hours. To permit children to follow company about, never giving them a moment of retirement, standing by while they make their toilet, is not only annoying, but is vulgar. (1859)

1879

THE considerate husband will never let his wife go to church alone on Sunday. (1892)

Entering the Church

Enter the church quietly, removing the hat, and never replacing it until the door is reached again at the close of the service. The gentleman will place his hat, if possible, under the seat. (1883)

Manners in Church

While in church avoid making a noise, staring around the building, whispering, laughing or nodding to others. All greetings, recognitions and conversation should be conducted in the vestibule after the service. (1883)

1893

Boorish Behavior

Gentlemen will not congregate in the vestibule or on the church steps to stare at the ladies as they pass out. Only boors do this. (1892)

Etiquette Quiz

Is it good form for a man to give a lady money to put in the contribution-box at church?

No; she is supposed to have her own funds for such purposes. (1889)

Don't Bustle

Arrive early and be seated in time. Don't bustle into a church after the commencement of the service. (1884)

Show No Contempt

Don't, if you go into a church or place of worship, show any contempt for the service. You are not obliged to go there, but if you do, you are bound to respect the feelings of others, and as nearly as possible follow the customs of regular worshipers. (1884)

1912 THE LONG SERMON —

A Strange Church

Don't, if you go to a strange church, decline to contribute to the offertory on the grounds that you do not like the service. (1884)

Dressing for Church

Well-bred people attend church in simple costumes, free from display. These may be of rich materials, but they are quiet in color and make. Jewelry, other than a simple pin, should not be used; earrings, of course, if one is in the habit of wearing them, but not diamonds. The church is not the place to flaunt elegant attire in the face of less fortunate worshipers in the "I-am-richer-than-thou" style. (1896b)

1878

Politeness in Church

Be in your seat before the services begin. Do not talk in church. Do not look at your watch during the service. Do not look around the congregation. It is not polite to do these things. Be quiet in church. Be ready to offer your seat and your book to a stranger. Do not use a fan to the annoyance of those near you. If you must fan yourself, do it very gently. (1900)

Clothes for Church

A policeman asked a poor child, "Where do you go to church, boy?" He answered, "We don't have no clothes to go to church, sir." (Collected by Jacob A. Riis, 1890)

Church Decorum

Do not fidget or move about in the pew, and never stare about at the congregation. Keep your eyes constantly on the minister. If you fancy his sermon tedious do not show this in your manner. It is the height of incivility to look at a watch during the sermon.

Etiquette Quiz
Is it proper to bow to a friend in church?

No. Greetings may only be exchanged in th vestibule at the close of the services. (1892)

Sapping Your Vitality

THE whole person must be kept scrupulously clean; but it must not be forgotten that the bath hath its dangers as well as its benefits. To bathe too often may be even worse than not to bathe at all; vitality often being sapped by over-indulgence in the lavatory. (1892)

1903

The Hair

The hair needs careful brushing both night and morning; and occasionally it should be cleansed with the yolk of an egg beaten, or with a mixture of lime juice and glycerine. (1892)

Offending The Olfactory Nerves

If the husband wishes to be held in pleasurable esteem by a sensitive and refined wife, or, if the wife hopes to retain the affections of a refined husband, each should avoid offending the olfactory nerves of the other. (1916)

Cleanliness is Next to Godliness.

Water is Cheap

Cleanliness and neatness are the invariable accompaniments of good breeding. Every gentleman may not be dressed expensively, he may not be able to do so; but water is cheap, and no gentleman will ever go into company unmindful of cleanliness either in his person or apparel. (1860)

> ### *Cleanliness always betokens refinement.* (*Scribner's Magazine*, 1894)

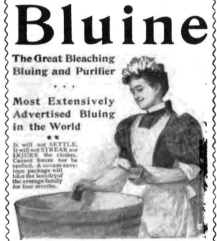

Bluine
The Great Bleaching Bluing and Purifier
· · ·
Most Extensively Advertised Bluing in the World
· ·
It will not SETTLE. It will not STREAK nor INJURE the clothes. Cannot freeze nor be spilled. A 10-cent envelope package will blue the laundry of the average family for four months.

Finest Laundry Bluing in the World
Sold Everywhere, or sent by mail from factory for 10 cents in stamps or silver
BLUINE COMPANY, - Concord Junction, Mass.

1900

Inner Cleanliness

It is your duty as an intelligent human being to be chaste and cleanly. Be as careful of the clothing of the mind as of the outward apparel. Let no smirch or smut soil the pure garments of thought. Be cleanly, inside and outside. Thus will you attain an honest, sterling character, of high moral excellence. (1894)

Smelly Persons

Bad smelling persons are exceedingly disagreeable companions. (1892)

A Pure Mind

No man who is uncleanly need expect to have a pure mind, nor to give a decent inheritance to a child. (1916)

When to Bathe

Very robust people may perhaps safely bathe twice a day in summer and once a day in winter. One of a weakly constitution should not venture to bathe oftener than once or twice a week. (1892)

Moral Beauty

Neither physical nor moral beauty can exist without cleanliness, which indicates self-respect, and is the root of many virtues, especially those of purity, modesty, delicacy and decency. (1899b)

Causing Indignation

ONE should by all possible means avoid egotism, for nothing is more displeasing and disgusting. Never make yourself the hero or heroine of your own story. Do not attempt a fine flight of language upon ordinary topics. To interrupt a person when speaking is the height of ill manners, and may justly cause indignation on the part of the one so interrupted. (1889)

Ill-bred people shout, shriek, and scream. They do not converse. (1910)

1889

Always look, but never stare, at those with whom you converse. (1881)

Points to Remember

- Do not attempt to speak with the mouth full.
- If you are flattered, repel it by quiet gravity.
- Do not whistle, loll about, scratch your head, or fidget with any portion of your dress while speaking. 'Tis excessively awkward, and indicative of low-breeding.
- Strictly avoid anything approaching the absence of mind. There can be nothing more offensive than a preoccupied vacant expression. (1869)

Buffoonery

Mimicry is the lowest and most ill-bred of all buffoonery. Swearing, sneering, private affairs either of yourself or any other, have long ago been banished out of the conversation of well-mannered people. (1869)

Whispering

Whispering is atrocious, and cannot be tolerated. Eschew scandal, for in scandal as in robbery, the receiver is always thought as bad as the thief. (1869)

1878

Lessons in Conversation

- Avoid satire and sarcasm.
- Avoid exaggeration.
- Never tell a coarse story.
- Be modest.
- Be what you wish to seem.
- Avoid repeating a brilliant or clever saying.
- Avoid oddity. Eccentricity is shallow vanity.
- Never discourse upon your ailments.
- Do not be too positive.
- Never prompt a slow speaker.
- Never mention your own peculiarities.

- Do not become a distributor of small talk in a community.
- Do not interrupt another when speaking.
- Do not find fault, though you may gently criticize.

1879

- Never utter an uncomplimentary word against any one.
- Do not appear to notice inaccuracies of speech in others.
- Do not talk of yourself or of your friends or your deeds.
- Do not always prove your self to be the one in the right.
- Sharp sayings are an evidence of low breeding.
- It is half of conversation to listen well. (1916)

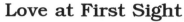

Love at First Sight

LOVE alone is a very uncertain foundation upon which to base wedlock. There should be something more than love between a man and woman before they venture upon the sea of matrimony. There ought to be a thorough acquaintance, a harmony of tastes and temperament and a deep-rooted esteem. Without these their ship will be without ballast and the waves may make a wreck of it before it fairly enters upon the long life voyage. (1892)

1894

In looking at young people we find our hearts, and almost our lips, crying out, "DON'T!" (1905)

Be Not Hasty

The young man who makes a proposal of marriage to a young lady on brief acquaintance is not only indiscreet but presumptuous. A woman who would accept a gentleman at first sight can hardly possess that discretion needed in a good wife and we therefore counsel the impetuous lover to restrain his ardor, thus avoiding the chances of disappointment. Discretion is as wise in love as it is in war. (1892)

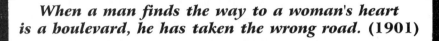

> *When a man finds the way to a woman's heart
> is a boulevard, he has taken the wrong road.* **(1901)**

Trifling With a Man's Feelings

Some young ladies pride themselves upon the conquests which they make, and would not scruple to sacrifice the happiness of an estimable person to their reprehensible vanity. Let this be far from you. If you see clearly that you have become an object of especial regard to a gentleman, and do not wish to encourage his addresses, treat him honorably and humanely, as you hope to be used with generosity by the person who may engage your own heart. Do not let him linger in suspense; but take the earliest opportunity of carefully making known your feelings on the subject. (1881)

1892

Spooning

Spooning is the popular name used by modern society for the indiscreet, suggestive and sentimental relations too often engaged in by young people. "There is a time for all things." Spooning has its rightful place in the economy of nature among fish, birds, animals and man. (1916)

Do Not Provoke Lovers' Quarrels

When a young lady encourages the addresses of a young man, she should behave honorably and sensibly. She should not lead him about as if in triumph, nor take advantage of her ascendancy over him by playing with his feelings. She should not seek occasions to tease him, as that may try his temper. Neither should she affect indifference, nor provoke a lovers' quarrel for the foolish pleasure of reconciliation. (1892)

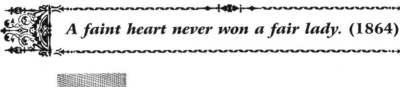

A faint heart never won a fair lady. **(1864)**

1912

The Clever Girl

A clever girl may usually marry any man she sees fit to honour with the responsibility of her bills. (1901)

Selecting a Wife

Some men select a wife as they would a horse, paying due attention to appearance, gait, disposition, age, teeth, and grooming. (1901)

Measure for Measure

Before tolerating the serious addresses of any man a women should feel that it is possible in time to return his affections, measure for measure. (1892)

The Domineering Lover

The lover who assumes a domineering attitude over his future wife invites her to escape from his tyranny while yet she may, and if she be wise she will escape, for the chances are that he will be worse as a husband than as a lover. (1892)

Marrying For Beauty

It is not wise to marry for beauty alone, as even the finest landscape, seen daily, becomes monotonous, so does the most beautiful face, unless a beautiful nature shine through it. The beauty of to-day becomes commonplace tomorrow; whereas goodness, displayed through the most ordinary features, is perennially lovely. (1886)

Where Dangers Lurk

Kissing, embracing, sitting on a lover's lap, leaning on his breast, long periods of secluded companionship are dangerous conditions. Thoughtful parents should have a profound fear at the dangers surrounding such a state of affairs. It is a marvel that so many ladies arrive safely at the wedding day. If our young women realized the danger of arousing the sexuality even of the best men, they would shudder at the risk they run. Don't do it, ladies! (1916)

1912

Don't Hesitate

When the young man is fully satisfied, and certain of the lady's regard for him, he should not hesitate. In justice to the lady, as well as himself, he should settle the matter by a manly, straight-forward offer of marriage. (1916)

Hands Off!

Dear girls, be happy, be merry, have all the harmless fun that the good God sends your way. But for the sake of the man who may one day seek you and win you — for the sake of the womanhood that he would honor — let all men know that you are labeled — "HANDS OFF!" and that you are not to be cheaply gained. (1905)

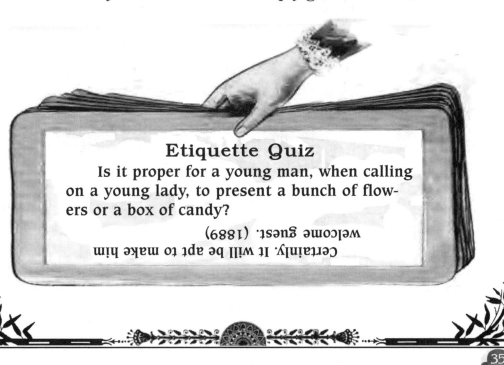

Etiquette Quiz

Is it proper for a young man, when calling on a young lady, to present a bunch of flowers or a box of candy?

Certainly. It will be apt to make him welcome guest. (1889)

The Coquette

It is a melancholy fact that some young women pride themselves upon their conquests, regardless of the mischief they have done to those whose hearts they have cruelly wounded. It is a shameful vanity, and no true woman will indulge in it. (1892)

1879

Should the Unmarried Spoon?

In the human family, spooning belongs only to the married life. If indulged in by married people beyond reasonable limits, it leads to sensuality, physical, mental and moral injury. If indulged in, even to a very limited extent among the single, it is fraught with gravest temptations. (1916)

May the Flame of Love never burn up the spark that kindled it. **(1860)**

How to Woo a Young Lady

If the individual be a timid damsel, do not frighten her; for this will drive away every vestige of lurking affection, and turn her faculties against you; but be gentle and soothing and offer her all the protection in your power, causing her to feel safe under your wing, and she will hover under it, and love you devoutly for the care you bestow upon her. (1864)

Why are lovers like armies? Because they get along well enough till the engagement begins.
(Frank Leslie's Pleasant Hours, 1885)

Dear Young Ladies

Young woman, I need not tell you to look out for your husband, for I know that you are fixing contrivances to catch one, and are as naturally on the watch as a cat is for a mouse. But one word in your ear, if you please. Don't bait your hook with an artificial fly of beauty; if you do, the chances are that you will catch a gudgeon — some silly fool of a fish that isn't worth his weight in sawdust. Array the inner lady with the beautiful garments of

1878

virtue, modesty, truth, morality, and unsophisticated love; and you will dispose of yourself quicker, to much better advantage than you would if you displayed all the gew-gaws, flippejigs, fol-derols, and fid- dle-de-dees in the universe. (1864)

Easy Does it, Gentlemen!

DANCE quietly; do not kick and caper about, nor sway your body to and fro; dance only from the hips downward; and lead the lady as lightly as you would tread a measure with a spirit of gossamer. (1843)

1883

*To all gentlemen, I would say; Learn to dance.
You will find it one of the best
plans for correcting bashfulness. (1875)*

How to Ask a Lady to Dance

In inviting a lady to dance with you, the words, "Will you honor me with your hand for a quadrille? "or, "Shall I have the honor of dancing this set with you?" are more used now than "Shall I have the pleasure?" or, "Will you give me the pleasure of dancing with you?" (1881)

Do Not Drag Her

Lead the lady through the quadrille; do not drag her, nor clasp her hand as if it were made of wood lest she not unjustly think you a boor. (1843)

Dancing

General Rules for a Ball-Room

A lady will not cross a ball-room unattended. A gentleman will not take a vacant seat next a lady who is a stranger to him. If she is an acquaintance, he may do so with her permission. White kid gloves should be worn at a ball, and only be taken off at supper-time. In dancing quadrilles do not make any attempt to take steps. A quiet walk is all that is required. When a gentleman escorts a lady home from a ball, she should not invite him to enter the house; and even if she does so, he should by all means decline the invitation. He should call upon her during the next day or evening. (1881)

A Lady at a Ball

At a ball, the lady should always be accompanied by a gentleman; it is quite improper to saunter around alone. (1859)

Girls Who Take the Lead

Girls who are addicted to the dance are accustomed to frequent personal contact with men. These girls are many times inclined to bestow favors. They sometimes invite familiarities. (1916)

Shun the Waltz

The waltz is a dance of quite too loose a character, and unmarried ladies should refrain from it altogether, both in public and private; very young married ladies, however, may be allowed to waltz in private balls, if it is very seldom, and with persons of their acquaintance. It is indispensable for them to acquit themselves with dignity and modesty. (1841)

1880

No Scowling, Please

The smile is essential. A dance is supposed to amuse, and nothing is more out of place than a gloomy scowl, unless it is an ill-tempered frown. (1875)

Easy Does It

A lady — a beautiful word! — is a delicate creature, one who should be reverenced and delicately treated. It is, therefore, unpardonable to rush around in a quadrille, to catch hold of a lady's hand as if it were a door-handle, or to drag her furiously across the room. (1875)

Wall Flowers

The master of the house should see that all the ladies dance; he should take notice, particularly of those who seem to serve as drapery to the walls of the ball-room, (or wall-flowers, as the familiar expression is,) and should see that they are invited to dance. (1881)

The round dance, waltz and tango are to be condemned on the same ground as spooning. **(1916)**

Only Dancers

Only those who dance should accept invitations to a ball. The presence of "wall-flowers" is not an honorable distinction which a hostess will crave. (1892)

Gross Familiarity

You should smile when you take a lady's hand. To squeeze it, on the other hand, is a gross familiarity, for which you would deserve to be kicked out of the room. (1875)

Dancing

Refusing to Dance

A lady cannot refuse the invitation of a gentleman to dance, unless she has already accepted that of another, for she would be guilty of an incivility which might occasion trouble; she would, moreover, seem to show contempt for him whom she refused, and would expose herself to receive in secret an ill compliment from the mistress of the house. (1881)

Forbidden Pleasure

Dancing — a simple, healthy, and useful exercise; a pleasant, social, and innocent amusement; a refined, elegant, and graceful accomplishment;

1880

and yet, because dancing has been abused, we find too many of our most conscientious and religious mothers forbidding its use entirely, and thus not only depriving their children of much rational enjoyment, but too often leading them into deceit and future excess in pursuit of a forbidden pleasure. (1868)

Attracting Attention

Dance with grace and modesty; neither affect to make a parade of your knowledge; refrain from great leaps and ridiculous jumps which would attract the attention of all towards you. (1841)

Becoming Noticed

A young lady should not dance with the same partner more than twice unless she desires to be noticed. (1892)

Be Punctual

1890

ELL-bred people arrive as nearly at the appointed dinner hour as they can. It is a very vulgar assumption of importance purposely to arrive half an hour behind time; besides the folly of allowing eight or ten hungry people such a tempting opportunity of discussing your foibles. (1843)

Thin Bread

At family dinners, where the common household bread is used, it should never be cut less than an inch and a half thick. There is nothing more plebeian than thin bread at dinner. (1843)

Dog Food

Squash, corn, beets, turnips, and tomato sauce, all on the same plate, remind one more of the contents a beggar's wallet, or a mess for a dog, than of a portion for a Christian gentleman. (1843)

Etiquette Quiz

Is it proper to use a knife and fork in eating asparagus, or should the stalks be taken in the fingers?

Never use a knife. Many well-bred people take the stalks in the fingers. (1889)

Picking Your Teeth

Avoid picking your teeth, if possible, at the table, for however agreeable such a practice might be to yourself, it may be offensive to others. The habit which some have of holding one hand over the mouth, does not avoid the vulgarity of teeth-picking at table. (1881)

Praising Every Dish

It is not good taste to praise extravagantly every dish that is set before you; but if there are some things that are really very nice, it is well to speak in their praise. But, above all things, avoid seeming indifferent to the dinner that is provided for you, as that might be construed into a dissatisfaction with it. (1881)

Don't Put on Airs

Avoid any air of mystery when speaking to those next to you; it is ill-bred and in excessively bad taste. (1875)

Home Cooked Meals

Good manners at dinner when dinner is just a home meal requires no squabbling, no quarrels, no finding a flaw in anything from soup to dessert. (1910)

No Gloves, Ladies

Ladies should never dine with their gloves on — unless their hands are not fit to be seen. (1843)

Dining

Shoveling

This is a besetting sin of Americans of all ranks. Nothing is more horrible than to witness a man make a shovel out of his knife, with the momentary expectation with seeing him cut his mouth with every throw. It is in itself an atrocity, that, in Europe, would shut him out of the pale of civilized life. (1843)

Unsociable Behavior

Solemn dullness and unsociability at meals is one of the national characteristics of Americans and cannot be too quickly rectified. (1843)

Dining Don'ts

- Don't, when you drink, elevate your glass as if you were going to stand it inverted on your nose, like some do.
- Don't tuck your napkin under your chin, nor spread it upon your breast. Bibs and tuckers are for the nursery.
- Don't mop your face or beard with your napkin. Draw it across your lips neatly.
- Don't decorate your shirt front with egg or coffee drippings, and don't ornament your coat-lapels with grease-spots. Few things are more distasteful than to see a gentleman bearing upon his apparel ocular evidence of his breakfast or his dinner. (1884)

Eating Corn

It is not elegant to *gnaw* Indian corn. The kernels should be scored with a knife, scraped off into the plate, and then eaten with a fork. Ladies should be particularly careful how they manage so particular a dainty, lest the exhibition rub off a little desirable romance. (1843)

ON'T fail to notice elderly people.

- Don't contradict people, even if you're sure you are right.
- Don't be inquisitive about the affairs of even your most intimate friend.
- Don't chew tobacco.
- Don't repeat gossip.
- Be what you wish to seem.
- Don't read to yourself in company.
- Don't walk with a slovenly gait.
- Don't be overfamiliar.
- Don't be rude to your inferiors in social positions.
- Don't overdress or underdress.
- Don't use hair dye, hair oil or pomades.
- Don't scold and snarl, as it is exceedingly ill-bred to do so.
- Don't carry your hands in your pockets.
- Don't go untidy on the plea that everybody knows you.
- Don't be vulgar, but don't show that you are trying hard not to be vulgar.

1897

- Don't try, when in company, to attract the attention of someone by signals, a cough or a nudge.
- Don't underrate anything because you don't possess it.
- Don't vent your irritation on anybody.
- Don't chew or fumble your toothpick in public.
- Don't beat the devil's tattoo with foot or fingers.
- Don't touch people when addressing them. (1916)

Entertaining at Home

HE Victor talking-machine is a valuable adjunct to the week-end party. A good instrument with the records of the best opera singers, now easily obtainable, the favorite waltzes and the latest thing from the vaudeville, adds to the gayety of the company and gives very little trouble. (1909c)

Fun At Home

Don't be afraid of fun at home, good people! Don't shut up your houses, lest the sun should fade your carpets; and your hearts, lest a hearty laugh should shake down some of the musty old cobwebs there! If you want to ruin your sons, let them think that all mirth and social enjoyment must be left on the threshold when they come home at night. (*Manford's Magazine, January,* 1890)

1897

1897

Late for the Party

"I'm afraid you'll be late at the party," said an old lady to her stylish granddaughter, who then replied, "Oh, you dear grandmother, don't you know in our fashionable 'set,' nobody ever goes to a party til everybody is there." (*Frank Leslie's Pleasant Hours,* 1878)

"THE PHONOGRAPH"

1905

Importance of Fashion

W E must imagine fashionable life as a great sea on which all crafts are sailing. Fashion means so much. It means pre-eminence among our kind, it is leadership, it is success, it is pleasure, it is gay delight, it is the front seat. (1884b)

The Low-Necked Dress

1890

The low-neck dress is a fatal lure to many a woman who ought to know better than to display her physical imperfections to the gaze of a pitiless world. Either a fat old woman or a scrawny young one should be wise enough to court the favoring and softening influences of high necks and any other devices for lessening the obviousness of their defects of form. (1892)

1909

Send Only

25c

$1.95

Buys this Pattern Hat

1903

Low-Necked Dresses

Girls who are fond of wearing very low-necked dresses, certainly ought to be informed that this is the most extreme and dangerous form of invitation. A reform in low-necked dressed is a moral necessity. (1916)

Nobody But My Husband

In America, some women think that anything is good enough to wear at home. They go about in slatternly morning dresses, unkempt hair, and slippers down at the heel. "Nobody will see me," they say, "but my husband." (1916)

How to Shave

THE chief requirements are hot water, a large, soft brush of badger hair, a good razor, soft soap that will not dry rapidly, and a steady hand. Cheap razors are a fallacy. They soon lose their edge, and no amount of stropping will restore it. A good razor needs no strop. If you can afford it, you should have a case of seven razors, one for each day of the week, so that no one shall be too much used (1875)

1896

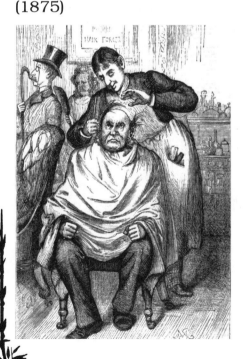

The Well-Kept Beard

The pride of a man is a handsome, well-kept beard. (1893)

Facial Defects

Almost every defect of face may be concealed by a judicious use and arrangement of hair. Take care, however, that your hair be not of one colour and your whiskers of another; and let your wig be large enough to cover the whole of your red or white hair. (1836)

Passing Muster

AVOID affecting singularity in dress. Expensive dressing is no sign of a gentlemen. If a gentleman is able to dress expensively it is very well for him to do so, but if he is not able to wear ten-dollar broadcloth, he may comfort himself with the reflection that cloth which costs but three dollars a yard will look quite as well when made into a well-fitting coat. With this suit, and well-made shoes, clean gloves, a white pocket-handkerchief, and an easy and graceful deportment withal, he may pass muster as a gentleman. Manners do quite as much to set off a suit of clothes as clothes do to set off a graceful person. (1860)

1891

A Good Toilet

A gentleman's dress should be so quiet and so perfect that it will not excite remark or attention. The suspicion of being dressed up defeats an otherwise good toilet. (1910)

The Well-Dressed Man

A snuff box, watch, studs, sleeve-buttons, watch-chain, and one ring are all the jewelry a well-dressed man can wear. (1875)

Morning Dress For Gentlemen

The morning dress for gentlemen is a black frock-coat, or a black cutaway, white or black vest, according to the season, gray or colored pants, plaid or stripes, according to the fashion, a high silk (stovepipe) hat. (1882)

THE SEVEN AGES OF MAN—PANTS

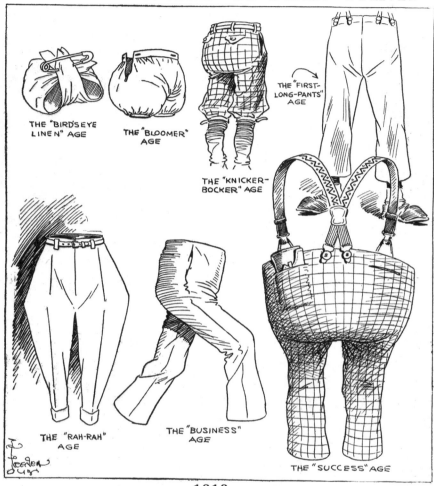

THE "BIRDSEYE LINEN" AGE

THE "BLOOMER" AGE

THE "KNICKERBOCKER" AGE

THE "FIRST-LONG-PANTS" AGE

THE "RAH-RAH" AGE

THE "BUSINESS" AGE

THE "SUCCESS" AGE

1912

What a True Gentleman Wears

Afternoon dress consists of a double-breasted frock coat of dark material, and waistcoat, either single or double-breasted, of same, or of some fancy material of late design. The trousers should be of light color, avoiding of course extremes in patterns. White or delicate color linen shirts should be worn, patent leather shoes, silk hat and undressed kid gloves of dark color. Afternoon dress is worn at weddings, afternoon teas, receptions, garden parties, luncheons, church funerals, and at all afternoon functions. (1904)

What is it to be a Gentleman?

T is to be honest, to be gentle, to be generous, to be brave, to be wise, and possessing all these qualities, to exercise them in the most graceful outward manner. Ought a gentleman to be a loyal son, a true husband, an honest father? Ought his life to be decent, his bills to be paid, his tastes to be high and elegant, his aim in life lofty and noble? In a word, ought not the biography of a First Gentleman in Europe be of such a nature that it might be read in young ladies' schools with advantage, and studied with profit in the seminaries of young gentlemen? (1846)

1878

The Duty of a Gentleman

It is the duty of a gentleman to know how to ride, to shoot, to fence, to box, to swim, to row, and to dance. He should be graceful. If attacked by ruffians, a man should be able to defend himself, and also defend women against their insults. (1893)

Frippery of the Dandy

Avoid what is called the "ruffianly style of dress," or the nonchalant and slouching appearance of a half unbuttoned vest and suspenderless pantaloons. That sort of affectation is, if possible, even more disgusting than the painfully elaborate frippery of the dandy. (1860)

1880

1878

The Bad Boy vs. The Good Boy

1891

A bad boy is one who steals or swears or lies, and a good boy one who is honest and pure and truthful. A bad boy has vices, bad habits; a good boy has virtues, good habits. The vices are the clothes worn on the bad boy's soul or heart; the virtues clothe the good boy's heart. (*The Expository Times*, 1898)

The Good Boy

Recently, some very bad boys tied an old tin can to a little black dog's tail, and he was afraid, but a little boy who was good caught the dog and got the can untied so the little dog didn't cry any more. That little boy was brave. (*The Century Illustrated Monthly Magazine*, 1901)

> ***Bad boys go to the bad world, and good boys go to Heaven. (Southern Reporter, 1909)***

INCORRIGIBLE.
1883

A Good Spanking

You cannot control a naturally obstinate boy unless he knows there is some force behind the orders directed against him. A good spanking will serve to make him avoid infractions of the school rules, because a boy will dodge not only the pain of the punishment but the humiliation that it entails. (*American Education*, 1905)

Good Boys, Bad Boys

A Week Before Christmas

1912

The Hard Nut

If a boy in a good home goes wrong he must by nature be a very bad boy. The naturally bad boy is a hard nut to crack. (*The Fortnightly Review*, 1897)

Truant Officers

Truant officers, whose watchful eyes are ever on the alert for bad boys, that they may be made good boys. (*Sunset Magazine*, 1906)

Advice From Uncle Tom's Cabin

"And now, Mas'r George," said Tom, "ye must be a good boy. Al'ays keep close to yer mother. Don't be gettin' into any of them foolish ways boys has of gettin' too big to mind their mothers. The Lord gives good many things twice over; but he don't give ye a mother but once. So, now, you hold on to her, and grow up, and be a comfort to her, thar 's my own good boy, — you will, now, won't ye? "Yes, I will, Uncle Tom," said George, seriously. (*Uncle Tom's Cabin* by Harriet Beecher Stowe, 1851)

 A real boy is worth half a dozen fops or dudes. (Manford's Magazine, 1885)

What is a Good Boy?

The good boy is one who does not smoke or fight, or play hooky. The good boy is one who minds his mother and does not quarrel. (*Education*, 1896)

1890

T is always the lady's privilege to extend the hand first. (1883)

Pitfalls of Handshaking

People who extend you one or two fingers or part of the hand only when they attempt to shake hands with you, expose unbounded egotism, ignorance, foolishness and serpentine hypocrisy ... A man who shakes a lady's hand with a tight squeeze and holds it unusually long will bear watching. (1889)

Offer the whole hand. It is an insult, and indicates snobbery, to present two fingers. (1883)

1883

When shaking hands. It is also insulting to return a warm, cordial greeting with a lifeless hand. (1883)

Present a cordial grasp and clasp the hand firmly, shaking it warmly for a period of two or three seconds, and then relinquish the grasp entirely. It is rude to grasp the hand very tightly or to shake it over-vigorously. To hold it a long time is often very embarrassing, and is a breach of etiquette. (1883)

Etiquette Quiz
If both parties are wearing gloves, is it necessary that each remove them in shaking hands?

No. However, if one has ungloved hands, it is courtesy for the other to remove the glove.

Hat Etiquette

DON'T forget to raise your hat to every lady acquaintance you meet, and to every gentleman you salute, when he is accompanied by a lady, whether you know her or not. (1884)

The hat is gracefully lifted from the head, brought to the level of the chest, and the body inclined forward, and then replaced in passing. (1904)

1896

Raising Your Hat

Men do not raise their hats to one another, save out of deference to an elderly person, a person of note, or a clergyman. (1904)

Remove Your Hat, Sir

A gentleman never sits in the house with his hat on in the presence of ladies for a single moment. Indeed, so strong is the force of habit, that a gentleman will quite unconsciously remove his hat on entering a parlor, or drawing-room, even if there is no one present but himself. People who sit in the house with their hats on are to be suspected of having spent the most of their time in barrooms and similar places. (1860)

1912

Hat Do's and Don'ts

Never nod to a lady in the street but take off your hat; it is a courtesy her sex demands. (1910)

If an individual of the lowest rank, or without any rank at all, takes his hat off to you, you should do the same in return. (1836)

In bowing to a woman it is not enough that you touch your hat; you must take it entirely off. (1836)

In driving, if impossible to raise the hat, he should touch it with his whip. (1904)

Etiquette Quiz
Is it rude for a man not to remove his hat when a lady enters an elevator?

If it is an office or business elevator, perhaps not. But the courtesy is always advisable; when in doubt, raise the hat. (1889)

Men and Their Old Hats

Women are said to have stronger attachments than men. It is not so. A man is often attached to an old hat; but did you ever know of a woman having an attachment for an old bonnet? Never! (*Frank Leslie's Pleasant Hours*, 1885)

Hat Flourishing

Elaborate hat-flourishing is often erroneously supposed to indicate "good manners." (Charles Dickens, *All Year Round*, 1884)

1876

Hat Etiquette When Cycling

Don't try to raise your hat to the passing "bloomer" until you become an expert in guiding your wheel. (1896b)

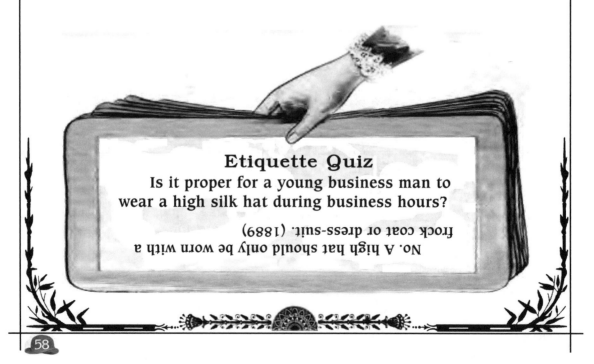

Etiquette Quiz

Is it proper for a young business man to wear a high silk hat during business hours?

No. A high hat should only be worn with a frock coat or dress-suit. (1889)

Softening of the Brain

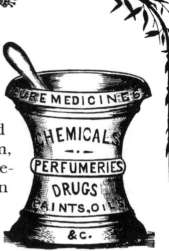

OBACCO lulls and dulls the sensibilities, blunts the moral nature. It is the next door neighbor to rum-drinking. It injures and disarranges the nervous system, makes those who use it cross, peevish, snappish and snarling, often paralyzing some part of the body, weakens energy of mind, and, in some cases, predisposes to softening of the brain. (1894b)

HOOD'S Sarsaparilla

MAKES PURE BLOOD
Cures Scrofula, Salt Rheum, All Humors,
Dyspepsia, Catarrh, Rheumatism

Undue Fear of Leeches

If you know persons who feel any disgust at leeches, do not be infected by their folly; but reason yourself into a more rational state of mind. Look at them as a curious piece of mechanism; remember, that although their office is an unpleasant one to our imagination, it is their proper calling, and that when they come to us from the apothecary, they are perfectly clean though slippery to the touch. Their ornamental stripes should recommend them even to the eye, and their valuable services to our feelings. (1836)

Three castor beans, strung on a silk thread and hung around your neck, will prevent cholera - if you draw the thread tight enough.
(Frank Leslie's Pleasant Hours, 1878)

Memories of Home

HERE is one vision that never fades from the soul, and that is the vision of mother and of home. No man in all his weary wanderings ever goes out beyond the overshadowing arch of home. (1916)

Home is...

• The father's kingdom, the children's paradise, the mother's world.

• The center of our affections, around which our heart's best wishes twine.

• A little hollow scooped out of the windy hill of the world, where we can be shielded from its cares and annoyances.

• The central telegraph office of human love, into which run innumerable wires of affection, many of them extending thousands of miles, but never disconnected from the one great terminus.

• The only place on earth where the faults and failings of humanity are hidden beneath a mantle of charity.

• The place where one is treated best and grumbles most. (1916)

Home is the woman's kingdom, and there she reigns supreme. (1882)

Home Sweet Home

There is a picture, bright and beautiful, but nevertheless true, where hearts are united for mutual happiness and mutual improvement; where a kind voice cheers the wife in her hour of trouble, and where the shade of anxiety is chased from the husband's brow as he enters his home; where sickness is soothed by watchful love, and hope and faith burn brightly. For such there is a great reward, both here and hereafter, in their own and their families' spiritual happiness and growth, and in the blessed scenes of the world of spirits. (1916)

1896

1883

Not to Strangers

Never give all your pleasant words and smiles to strangers. The kindest words and the sweetest smiles should be reserved for home. Home should be our heaven. (1883)

No Home for a Bachelor

There cannot be a home where there is no wife. To talk of a home without love, we might as well expect to find a New England fireside in one of the pyramids of Egypt. (1894)

Inviolate Secrets

ALL details of the honeymoon should be arranged beforehand by the best man, who knows the destination, and should keep it an inviolate secret, revealing it only in case of accident. (1904)

A Thing of the Past

It is becoming the fashion for the married couple to do away with the trip, and instead to begin their married life in their own home. (1904)

1892

A Bride's Tasks

A bride is not expected to begin her lifelong task of darning stockings and sewing on buttons until the honeymoon has become a thing of the past. (1910)

Tiresome Quiet

It would be mere cruelty to expect a fashionable bride to waste a month in a honeymoon of tiresome quiet at some dull spot. (1887)

> *A nobleman, who was about to marry a lady of great fortune, was asked one day at dinner, how long he thought honeymoon would last, and replied, "Don't talk of honeymoon, it is harvest-moon with me."* (1860)

Hotel Manners

A Hotbed of Gossip

T is a well-known fact that there is no other hotbed of gossip equal to a hotel or a boarding-house. Women, released from the cares and anxieties of housekeeping and home-making, turn their time and thoughts to fancy work and scandal. Each arrival runs the gauntlet of criticism and comment, and afterward becomes the subject of "confidential" conversations upon veranda and in parlors. (1905)

Ladies at a Hotel

No lady should use the piano of a hotel uninvited if there are others in the room. It looks bold and forward to display even the most finished musical education in this way. It is still worse to sing. (1910)

1878

Three gentlemen, going into a hotel together, one said to the waiter, " Bring me a glass of brandy-and-water, I am so hot!" Another said, " Bring me some gin-and-sugar; I have just had a chill." The other cried out, "Bring me a rum-punch, because I Like it." (1860)

How to Choose a Husband

The Model Husband

A young woman should be able to find in the husband of her choice honor, purity, strength and courage. (1916)

Find His Defects

A young woman should take pains to find out the defects and weaknesses of the man who would make her his life companion, for defects he will have, else he is not of the earth. (1916)

1897

Don't Go to it Blind

You would not like to live with a liar, with a thief, with a drunkard, for twenty or thirty years. (1886)

The Lazy Man

A lazy man will make but a weak band of support for his and your house; so will one deficient in fortitude — that is, the power to bear pain and trouble without whining. (1886)

1867

Avoid the Genius

Never marry a genius. As the supply of geniuses is very limited, this advice may seem superfluous. It is not so, however, for there is enough and to spare of men who think that they are geniuses, and take liberties accordingly. (1886)

Men to Shun

Appearances are often deceptive. A young lady should take no chances. Through some discreet friend, she should investigate her lover's habits. If his record is not clear, better let him go. No man who drinks, or swears, or gambles, or associates with lewd persons, is fit to become the husband of a pure woman. Any woman who marries such a man is selling herself into bondage. (1916)

The Selfish Man

Beware of the selfish man, for though he may be drawn out of selfishness in the early weeks of courtship, he will settle back into it again when the wear and worry of life come on. (1886)

Beware the Effeminate Face

Girls and women, beware of men with effeminate faces, for, as a rule, they lack moral character, and are deceitful and untrustworthy in the highest degree. (1892b)

A reformed rake makes the best husband. (1859b)

1883

THE girl who brings to her husband a large dowry may also bring habits of luxury learned in a rich home. (1886)

The Ideal Wife

What men want for the most part is a humble, nattering, smiling, child-loving, tea-making being, who laughs at our jokes however old they may be, coaxes and wheedles us in our humours, and fondly lies to us through life. (1886)

How to Choose a Wife

Characteristics of Woman

There is beauty in the helplessness of woman. The clinging trust which searches for extraneous support is graceful and touching. Timidity is the attribute of her sex; but to herself it is not without its dangers, its inconveniences, and its sufferings. Her first effort at comparative freedom is bitter enough; for the delicate mind shrinks from every unaccustomed contact and the warm and gushing heart closes itself, like the blossom of the sensitive plant, at every approach. (1916)

Le Breton
1903

Nothing is better than a good woman,
nor anything worse than a bad one. **(1916)**

Why Men Should Marry

"If you are for pleasure, marry; if you prize rosy health, marry. A good wife is Heaven's last and best gift to man, his angel of mercy. Her voice is his sweetest music; her smile his brightest day; her kiss the guardian of his innocence; her industry his surest wealth; her economy his safest steward; her lips his faithful counselors; her bosom his safest pillow, her prayer his ablest advocate of Heaven's court." Bishop Taylor (1892)

1883

What Men Need Wives For

It is not to sweep the house and make the beds and darn the socks and cook the meals, chiefly, that a man needs a wife. If this is all he wants, hired servants can do it cheaper than a wife. What the true man most wants of a wife is her companionship, sympathy and love. The way of life has many dreary places in it and man needs a companion to go with him. (1916)

How to Choose a Wife

Love is Blind

The young man should not be so blinded by the young lady's charms that he can not study her personal habits closely. Notice her teeth, neck, hair and nails. Her clothes must be clean and neat, especially collars and cuffs, and the like. She should be orderly in her habits; and the young man is wise who discovers, accidently, of course, how she keeps her own room and belongings. If she's a cheerful helpful about the house, good to her mother, and can get up an appetizing square meal out of "scraps," she's a jewel worth winning. (1916)

1900

Beauty is Only Skin Deep

The important thing to do is to keep well in mind the fact that a man's prospect of domestic felicity does not depend upon the face, the fortune, or the accomplishments of his wife, but upon her character. (1886)

A man should marry to obtain a friend and companion rather than a cook and housekeeper. (1886)

Choosing a Wife

Young man, a word in your ear, when you choose a wife. Don't be fascinated with a dashing creature, fond of society, vain, artificial, and showy in dress. You do not want a doll or a coquette for a partner. Choose rather one of those retiring, modest, sensible girls, who have learnt to deny themselves, and possess some decided character. But above all, seek for a good disposition. No trait of character is more valuable in a female than the possession of a sweet temper. Home can never be made happy without it. (1864)

Witticisms

D O not be always witty, even though you should be so happily gifted as to need the caution. To out shine others on every occasion is the surest road to unpopularity. (1881)

Punning

Punning is now decidedly out of date. It is a silly and displeasing thing, when it becomes a habit. Someone has called it the wit of fools. It is within the reach of the most trifling, and it is often used by them to puzzle and degrade the wise. Whatever may be its merits, it is now out of fashion. (1836)

Proverbs and Puns

The use of proverbs is equally vulgar in conversation; and puns, unless they rise to the rank of witticisms, are to be scrupulously avoided. There is no greater nuisance in society than a dull and persevering punster. (1881)

1896

A Coarse Laugh

"A coarse laugh is a great blemish in either girl or woman. (*The People's Home Journal, April,* 1907.)

1896

Chivalric Regard

NOT his own convenience and pleasure alone, but the wife's, must be consulted, kindness and delicate attention are her due, and words and acts must be considered with chivalric regard for her gentle feelings and sensibilities. (1892)

Duties of the Husband

The burden, or, rather the privilege, of making home happy is not the wife's alone. There is something demanded of the lord and master and if he fails in his part, domestic misery must follow. (1892)

Self-Control

When small disputes arise, the husband will forbear. The wife's good sense must be given a chance to assert itself; and it is the man's prerogative to be strong. The husband who fails to master his own temper cannot hope to master that of his wife. (1892)

Share the Wealth

The plain duty of the husband is to make a frank statement of his income to his wife. Otherwise she cannot properly regulate her expenses and he will be constantly in fear lest she pass the limit of his ability to pay. (1892)

As Much as a Camel

Seclusion begets morbidness. She needs some of the life that comes from contact with society. She must see how other people appear and act. It often requires an exertion for her to go out of her home, but it is good for her, and for you. She will bring back more sunshine. It is wise to rest sometimes. When the Arab stops for his dinner he unpacks his camel. Treat your wife with as much consideration. (1880)

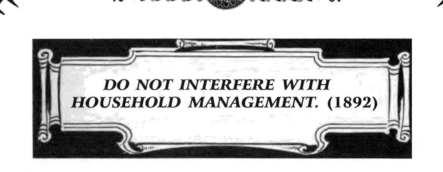

DO NOT INTERFERE WITH HOUSEHOLD MANAGEMENT. (1892)

The Home Department

The less the husband interferes with her management of the household the better it will be. The home department belongs to the wife exclusively; the husband's province is to rule the house — hers to regulate its internal economy. (1892)

The Way My Mother Did It

Do not indulge in invidious comparisons. Your mother and sisters were undoubtedly superior in household arts, but forbear to mention the fact. Many a wife has been alienated from her husband's family by injudicious and ungenerous references to "the way mother did it" and the man who thus wounds a tender and susceptible heart is unworthy of its devotion. (1892)

It's Your Fault

Most women are naturally amiable, gentle and compliant; and if a wife becomes perverse and indifferent to her home it is generally her husband's fault. (1892)

1900

Helpful Hints

- Do not put your feet on the chair and go to sleep.
- If she loves music, take her to the concert as you were wont to do when you sought her for a bride. (1892)

Husbandly Duties

The Paradise of Marriage

It is the paradise of marriage that the man should work for the woman; that he alone shall support her, take pleasure in enduring fatigue for her sake, and spare her the hardships of labor, and rude contact with the world.

He returns home in the evening, harassed, suffering from toil, mental or bodily, from the weariness of worldly things, from the baseness of men. But in his reception at home there is such an infinite kindness, a calm so intense, that he hardly believes in the cruel realities he has gone through all day. "No," he says, that could not have been; it was but an ugly dream." (1892)

Man's business is to earn money, hers to spend it. (1892)

The Wife Alone

It must not be supposed that it devolves upon the wife alone to make married life and home happy. She must be seconded in her noble efforts by him who took her from her own parental fireside and kind friends, to be his companion through life's pilgrimage. (1882)

The Capable Wife

The cares and anxieties of business should not exclude the attentions due to wife and family, while he should carefully keep her informed of the condition of his business affairs. Many a wife is capable of giving her husband important advice about various details of his business. (1882)

1897

Bungled Introductions

NTRODUCTIONS are often bungled in a most distressing manner. The well-meaning person who undertakes the office becomes confused, forgets the names, or does or says some awkward thing that increases his embarrassment. (1892)

Superiors and Inferiors

When introducing two gentlemen, you should look first to the elder, or, if there is a difference in social standing, to the superior, and with a bow say to him, "Mr. Jones, permit me to introduce to you my friend, Mr. Smith; then turn to Mr. Smith and say, "Mr. Smith, Mr. Jones." If either of the gentlemen have a title, do not fail to use it. (1892)

Introducing a Woman

No woman should allow a man to be introduced to her unless her permission has been first obtained. (1904)

Two Americans

When two Americans, who "have not been introduced," meet in some public place, as in a theatre, a stagecoach, or a steamboat, they will sit for an hour staring in one another's faces, but without a word of conversation. (1836)

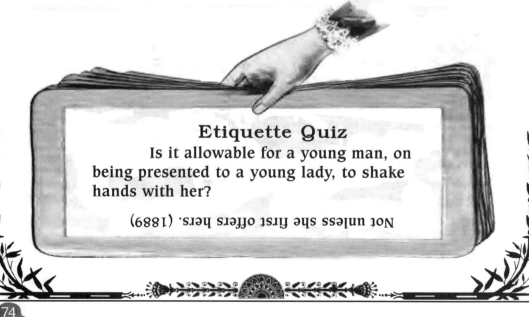

Etiquette Quiz
Is it allowable for a young man, on being presented to a young lady, to shake hands with her?

Not unless she first offers hers. (1889)

Introductions

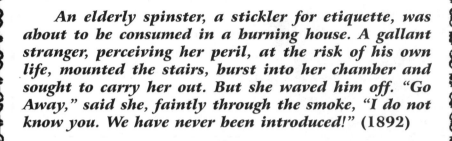

An elderly spinster, a stickler for etiquette, was about to be consumed in a burning house. A gallant stranger, perceiving her peril, at the risk of his own life, mounted the stairs, burst into her chamber and sought to carry her out. But she waved him off. "Go Away," said she, faintly through the smoke, "I do not know you. We have never been introduced!" (1892)

Who?

When you are introduced to a person, be careful not to appear as though you had never heard of him before. If he happens to be a person of any distinction, such a mistake would be unpardonable, and no person is complemented by being reminded of the fact that his name is unknown. (1860)

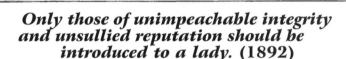

Only those of unimpeachable integrity and unsullied reputation should be introduced to a lady. (1892)

1877

Invitations

A LL invitations, save those to a dinner, are issued in the name of the lady of the house. Dinner invitations are issued in the names of both the host and hostess. (1892)

Answering Invitations

Never fail to answer an invitation, either personally or by letter, within a week after the invitation is received. (1883)

Invitations to a Ball

Persons giving balls or dancing parties should be careful not to invite more than their rooms will accommodate, so as to avoid a crush. Invitations to crowded balls are not hospitalities, but 1893 inflictions. A hostess is usually safe, however, in inviting one-fourth more than her rooms will hold, as that proportion of regrets are apt to be received. (1882)

Too Punctual

There is never any danger of being too punctual in replying to an invitation, and those who delay through fear of being deemed too eager to accept, act very foolishly. (1889d)

1880

Women Kissing in Public

USTOM seems to give a kind of sanction to women kissing each other in public; but there is, nevertheless, a touch of vulgarity about it, and a lady of really delicate perceptions will avoid it. (1881)

The Wedding Kiss

The kiss in the wedding ceremony is being done away with, especially at church weddings. Only the bride's parents and her most intimate friends should kiss her, and for others to do so is no longer good form. (1904)

Too Much Kissing

We kiss too much. The principles of both hygiene and honesty are constantly violated in the practice. We might well dispense with the perfunctory little peck on the cheek that means nothing, and reserve the kiss for the real embrace of affection. It ought not to be necessary — but it is — to say that kissing in public is extremely bad form. (1907)

1879

Irresistible Impulses

It would be well if every person in society should register a solemn resolution never to kiss anybody unless prompted to do so by the irresistible impulse of affection. It is safe to say that nine-tenths of the kisses of social greeting would be dispensed with. The quality of the remaining tenth would doubtless be proportionately improved. (1893b)

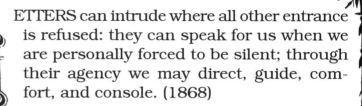

ETTERS can intrude where all other entrance is refused: they can speak for us when we are personally forced to be silent; through their agency we may direct, guide, comfort, and console. (1868)

Plain Paper

For notes, invitations and ordinary correspondence, plain paper is always preferable to the fancy styles that come and go in fashion. Ruled paper is allowable only in business correspondence. But for those whose lines have an uphill or down-hill tendency, it is better to write even small notes on ruled sheets than to invite criticism by the other fault. (1892)

Sealing with Wax

Sealing letters 1893 with wax is again in favor, but it should be adopted only by those who have learned how to make a clean, even, clearly marked seal. A slovenly seal is intolerable. (1892)

Breaking an Engagement by Letter

It is generally best to break an engagement by letter. By this means one can express himself or herself more clearly, and give the true reasons for his or her course much better than in a personal interview. (1868)

Letters

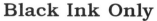

Black Ink Only

Use only black ink. Purple ink was in great favor some years ago but is no longer so. Plain black is now preferred by persons of taste, and, like good white paper, is really always in fashion. Of course none but country lads and lasses ever use red or blue inks. (1892)

Angry Letters

Avoid the pen as you would the Devil, when you are angry. If you must commit follies, don't put them down on paper. (1887)

1883

Bad Form

To use ruled paper for writing invitations is considered very "bad form." Ruled paper should be kept for business communications only. Those who have not learned to write straight must content themselves with using lines under their paper. The forms and colors of note-paper are so constantly changing and shifting, that it is hard to lay down any lasting rules in regard to styles. But it is always safe to choose plain, substantial paper, either white or of some light tint, and to avoid bright or striking colors, eccentric shapes. (1887)

Love Letters

For a love letter, good paper is indispensable. When it can be procured, that of a costly quality, gold-edged, perfumed, or ornamented in the French style, may be properly used. The letter should be carefully enveloped, and nicely sealed with a fancy wafer or, what is better, plain or fancy sealing wax. The whole affair should be as neat and elegant as possible. (1864)

1897

A Happy Workplace

THE maid sees in the mistress a possible tyrant, one who will exact the pound of flesh, and, if the owner thereof be not on her guard, will insist on a few extra ounces thrown in for good measure. The mistress sees in the suspicious girl a person who will, if the chance be offered her, turn against her employer, will do the smallest amount of work possible for the highest wages she can demand; break china, smash glass, shut her eyes to dirt in the corners, and accept the first opportunity that offers itself to leave her present place and get one that demands fewer duties and larger pay. (1905)

1889

Husband trying to look disinterested while hiring a new maid.

A Slovenly Household

Neatness is indispensable; a slovenly and inattentive servant betrays a slovenly household. (1912)

1912

Boss of the House

"Woman's RIGHTS!" exclaimed a man, when the subject was broached. "What more rights do they want? My wife is eternally bossing me, our daughters boss us both, and the servant-girl bosses the whole family. It's time the men were allowed some rights!" (*Frank Leslie's Pleasant Hours,* 1885)

The Tone of the Home

Servants are very apt to take their cue from their employers — to be civil if these are civil, and insolent if these are insolent. The tone of the head of the house is very apt to be copied and exaggerated by his flunkies. (1912)

Ruler of the House

It is a rare thing to see persons who are not controlled by their servants. Theirs, too, is not the only kitchen cabinet which begins by serving and ends by ruling. (1836)

1897

All But Impossible

The woman who employs one maid-of-all-work, and then demands that she shall be a superior cook, laundress, waitress, parlormaid and chambermaid, is an impossible mistress to suit. (1896c)

Marriage

Proposals by Women

PROPOSALS by women, while permissible, are not customary, and, although they are yearly becoming more and more popular, are still regarded as an innovation. If the proposal is rejected, good taste and kindly consideration demand that the gentleman should keep it more or less of a secret. (1908)

Marriage and Health

Statistics show that married men live longer than bachelors. Married, child-bearing women live longer than spinsters. Wives also have better health than their unmarried sisters. This, too, in spite of the added dangers associated with childbirth. Many delicate and ailing women have become robust during the rest of their lives after marriage and the birth of one or more children. (1916)

1883

"If compelled to choose, I would bestow my daughter upon a man without money sooner than upon money without a man."
Themistocles (1892)

Rules Governing Marriage

1880

- Marry in your own grade in society.
- Do not marry downward.
- Do not sell yourself. It matters not whether the price be money or position.
- Do not throw yourself away. You will not receive too much even if you are paid full price.
- Beware of mere magnetism.
- Do not marry simply because you have promised to do so.
- Do not marry the wrong object.
- Require brains. Culture is good, but will not be transmitted. Brain power may be.
- Study past relationships. The good daughter and sister makes a good wife. The good son and brother makes a good husband.
- Beware of one who has been intemperate.
- Marry character. It is not so much what one has as what one is.
- See where the candidate is going. (1880)

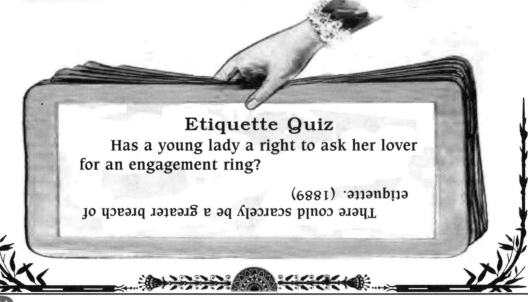

Etiquette Quiz
Has a young lady a right to ask her lover for an engagement ring?

There could scarcely be a greater breach of etiquette. (1889)

Marriage

Marriage Dont's

- Don't sell yourself for money or position.
- Don't throw yourself away; remember marriage is not for a day.
- Don't fail to seek the advice of your parents.
- Don't marry to please a third party.
- Don't marry to spite anyone.
- Don't marry because someone else is seeking the same person.
- Don't marry to get rid of anyone.
- Don't marry merely from the impulse of love.
- Don't marry without love.
- Don't marry simply because you have promised to do so.
- Don't fail to consider the effects of heredity on your children.
- Don't marry suddenly.
- Don't fail to consider the grade of the one you are to marry.
- Don't marry downward. (1916)

> *Because you are married is no excuse*
> *for neglecting your personal appearance.*
> **(Sears Roebuck catalog, 1910)**

Look Before You Leap

A man who has ruined the body and broken the spirit of one wife, and who seeks another with the same intentions, will certainly be left sometime somewhere to work out his own salvation. The woman who has foolishly or unwittingly married such an one, must also look out for herself, and she cannot secure peace while living in hell. (*The Ladies World*, June, 1897)

1880

Don't Look Down

Marry a person who is your equal in social position. If there be a difference either way let the husband be superior to the wife. It is difficult for a wife to love and honor a person whom she is compelled to look down upon. (1910)

Advice for Young Ladies

You are both young and it is best to be patient and let matters drift, rather than try to force them. Above all, do not make advances yourself, for nothing frightens away the average man like a wooing maiden. It may be that while the young man is fond of you, he does not wish to tie himself or you by a long engagement. Girls do not realize what a responsibility marriage places upon a man. (*The People's Home Journal*, April 1907)

The Business of Life

Matrimony for women is the great business of life, whereas with men, it is only an incident. (1838)

Familiarity Breeds Contempt

When husband and wife have become thoroughly accustomed to each other — when all the little battery of charms which each play off so skillfully before the wedding day has been exhausted — too many seem to think that nothing remains but the clanking of the legal chains which bind them to each other. (1916)

Better to have a fortune in your wife than with her. (1886)

Dress for Your Husband

Have the comfort and happiness of your husband always in view, and let him see and feel that you still look up to him with trust and affection — that the love of other days has not grown cold. Dress for his eyes more scrupulously than for all the rest of the world; make yourself and your home beautiful for his sake; try to beguile him from his cares; retain his affections in the same way that you won them. Be polite even to your husband. (1916)

1883

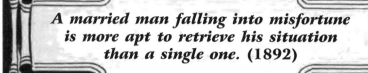

A married man falling into misfortune is more apt to retrieve his situation than a single one. (1892)

1912

Why Well-Disposed Wives Fail

Why is it that so many men are anxious to get rid of their wives? Because so few women exert themselves after marriage to make their presence indispensable to the happiness of their husbands. (1916)

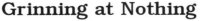

Grinning at Nothing

ON'T have the habit of smiling or "grinning" at nothing. Smile or laugh when there is occasion to do either, but at other times keep your mouth shut and your manner composed. (1884)

Over Familiarity

Don't be over-familiar. Don't strike your friends on the back, nudge them in the side, or give other physical manifestations of your pleasure. Don't indulge in these familiarities nor submit to them by others. (1884)

Eating a Banana

The skin should be cut off with a knife, peeling from the top down, while holding in the hand. Small pieces should be cut or broken off, and taken in the fingers, or they may be cut up and eaten with a fork. (1904)

1877

Treatment of Inferiors

Never affect superiority. If you chance to be in the company of an inferior, do not let him feel his inferiority. When you invite an inferior as your guest, treat him with all the politeness and consideration you would show an equal. (1893)

Too Nice

Be careful not to be over-nice, or you will impress people with the idea that your life began in vulgarity, and you are now trying so hard to get away from it, that you rush to the opposite extreme. (1860)

Shun The Gambler

Young man, beware of gambling and gamblers. They lead to evil, and to evil continually. Shun the whole brood of chance amusements. They are Satan's trap to catch souls. (*The Guardian,* 1867)

1912

The Country Bumpkin

A country bumpkin seizes your hand with as much violence as though he were catching a pig, and if he does not break your fingers it is a mercy. The fop languidly gives you his hand, and you may shake it if you will, but it cannot be said that he grasps yours. (1860)

The Nursery of Crime

Idleness is the nursery of crime. It is that prolific germ of which all rank and poisonous vices are the fruits. It is the source of temptation. (1894)

Timeless

It is not considered fashionable to carry a watch. What has a fashionable man to do with time? Besides, he never goes into those obscure parts of the town where there are no public clocks, and his servant will tell him when it is time to dress for

1903

dinner. A gentleman carries his watch in his pantaloons with a plain black ribbon attached. It is only worthy of a shop-boy to put it in his waistcoat pocket. (1836)

The Barbarous Banjo

Once, the banjo was considered a barbarous instrument, to be classed with the kettle-drum and tom-tom. Nowadays, the development of musical tastes have brought about an appreciation of the higher possibilities of the banjo. It is quite easy to learn and serves admirably to accompany singing in the parlor. (New York Times, November, 1883)

1891

Avoid the Horse-Laugh

Immoderate laughter is exceedingly unbecoming in a lady; she may affect the dimple or the smile, but should carefully avoid any approximation to a horselaugh. (1860)

The Spendthrift

BE sure you do not spend your money just for the sake of showing how liberal you are. Economy is nothing to be ashamed of. Avoid the habit of so-called treating. The habit is a bad one and is closely allied with loafing and dissipation. (1889b)

Allowances

To be taught early the real value of money is a distinct assistance to financial integrity in later life.

To have in one's possession, even as a child, a sum wholly one's own, conduces to a feeling of self-respect and independence. As soon as a child is old enough to know what money is and that, for money, things are bought and sold, he should have an allowance, be it only

1880

a penny a week. Suggestions, but not commands, as to its expenditure should accompany the gift. (1905)

A bankrupt gentleman declared before a commissioner that his available assets included a great number of debts. (Frank Leslie's Pleasant Hours, 1885)

Moral Fiber

The morals of our bank cashiers and our great army of embezzlers show what are the results of the want of proper moral training. (1887)

Restive Horses

RIVE slowly past any one driving or riding a restive horse and, if necessary, especially if it should be a lady or child riding or driving, stop the engine. (1909)

It's Not Your Fault

It lies with drivers to keep clear of pedestrians. All persons have a right to walk on the highways at their own pace. Dogs, chickens and other domestic animals at large on the highway are not pedestrians, and if one is driving at a regulation speed, or under, one is not responsible for their untimely end. (1909)

Sound Your Hooter

Do not fail to sound the hooter and slacken speed when coming to a crossroad, side-turning or bend. Many accidents may be averted by taking this precaution. A hooter is meant to give warning, not to startle people or wake up sleeping inmates in their houses at all hours. Remember, however, that it is necessary to sound the hooter when coming up behind and intending to pass a pedestrian or a vehicle. (1909)

> *If every woman and man who drove a car followed these suggestions there would not be an outcry against the motor-car.* (1909)

Motoring Manners

Cranking Your Car

Step briskly forward in front of the car, seize the handle that you will notice hanging there, and turn it sharply round from left to right. Then let go, and it will swing back and catch you a smart blow on the side of the head. Repeat the operation until the engine is started. You must, however, be careful to see that the brakes are on before you set the machinery going. Otherwise, of course, the car will start while you are winding it up, and you will be borne firmly but rapidly along into the window of the nearest greengrocer's shop, where

1909

a crate full of ripe bananas will impinge upon your solar plexus, possibly with fatal results.

When the engine is fairly started, run round and spring lightly into the car, pull back the handle you will see on the right-hand side and grasp the steering wheel. The rest must be left to Providence. (1910)

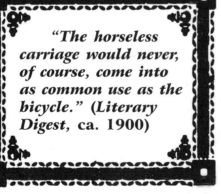

"The horseless carriage would never, of course, come into as common use as the bicycle." (Literary Digest, ca. 1900)

Motoring Manners

Tips for Motoring

1. Don't overload it. Was it built for two people? Then don't try to put four on it, although it will carry them.

2. Don't drive it continually at its highest speed, which is probably about thirty miles per hour. It strains the engine, which will do its best work at about twenty miles an hour, with an occasional spurt if you want it.

3. Keep it well cleaned. A little motor-car is ugly and noisy enough; a dirty little motor-car is a disgrace to its owner.

4. Use only the best oil and spirit, and never start out, if only for a ten-mile drive, without a full supply of both.

5. Never forget that your little car is not a big car. (1906)

Benefits of The Steam Car

There is a vague general impression that steam cars are obsolete. For the moment, they are not the fashion, but are very far indeed from being obsolete; they are extremely efficient; they have (unlike the petrol car) become simpler instead of more complicated; they are strongly built and sweet and silent in running; and for certain purposes they are still the most suitable form of self-propelled vehicle. The smoothness of their running makes for economy in up keep, as the shaking and vibration in-

Locomobile Two-Seat Steam Car, 1902

cidental to the use of an explosive engine are avoided. Steam cars have certain mild disabilities — such as the necessity for watchfulness in driving, in lubrication, and because of the presence of a fire — that tend to restrict their use to moderate journeys instead of hurried and, in the end, expensive long-distance non-stop runs. Their chief disadvantage is the necessity for carrying about with one a lighted fire; but on the newer cars this arrangement has been robbed of its former terrors, and one hardly ever hears of a conflagration on a steam car now. (1906)

1909

No Talking!

The well-known rule about "not speaking to the man at the wheel" holds good on the high road as well as on the high seas. I do not mean that one should not occasionally address a word of intelligent sympathy to the individual who is driving the car; but it is wrong to ply him with a ceaseless flow of reminiscent babble. It is, in fact, extremely dangerous to choose a moment when he is turning a sharp corner to point out certain beauties of the surrounding landscape which might otherwise possibly escape his notice. (1910)

The first thing necessary for the full enjoyment of motoring is the possession of a reliable chauffeur. (1910)

Hold Your Emotions in Check

Whatever happens, it is wrong for the motor passenger to express emotion of any kind, either by facial contortions or bodily wrigglings. When, in your opinion, the car has taken a corner at excessive speed, it is useless to writhe or give vent to your feelings in a loud whistling sigh of relief. (1910)

WHAT A DIFFERENCE IN A FEW YEARS

GOING TO CHURCH —
- 1871 -

-1912-

When you first get a car, don't be stingy.
Give the neighbors at least a smell of it. **(1906b)**

Avoid the Pitchfork!

If the situation is one of imminent danger — if a hay-cart containing a comatose yokel emerges from a side-road at the bottom of a steep hill, at the very moment when the chauffeur has discovered that his brakes are not working — it is simply futile to throw your arms round the driver's neck, burst into tears, and scream loudly. Such action only tends to obscure the view of the man at the wheel. The thing to do on such an occasion is to select a spot in the hay-cart where you may alight with the least possible physical discomfort (avoiding, if possible, the person of the comatose yokel and the pitchfork which he is in the habit of carrying), and then let Nature take its course. (1910)

Hundreds of Women Drivers

If a woman wants to learn how to drive and to understand a motor-car, she can and will learn as quickly as a man. Hundreds of women have done and are doing so, and there is many a one whose keen eyes can detect, and whose deft fingers can remedy, a loose nut or a faulty electrical connection in half the time that the professional chauffeur would spend upon the work. (1909)

1909

Single-Cylinder Car

If you are going to attend to the mechanism yourself, you should purchase a single-cylinder car — more cylinders mean more work, and also more expense as regards tyres, petrol, oil, etc. The single-cylinder car is the most economical to run. (1909)

Starting the Car

In front of the car you will notice a handle. Push it inwards until you feel it fit into a notch, then pull it up sharply, releasing your hold of the handle the moment you feel you have pulled it over the resisting (compression) point. On no account press down the handle — always pull it upwards, smartly and sharply. If it is pressed down the possibility of a back-fire is greater — and a broken arm may result. The moment the engine is running you can get in the car and start driving. (1909)

THE **Gasmobile**

PRICE $1,600.

The Finest Gasoline Touring Carriage Built in America.

AUTOMOBILE COMPANY OF AMERICA,
32 BROADWAY, NEW YORK.

1900

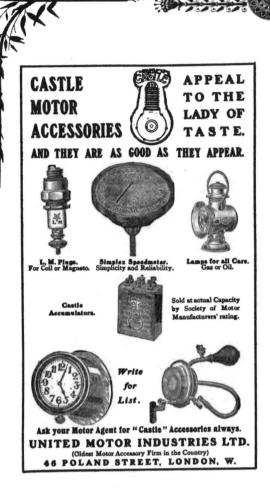
Useful Accessories

There are numberless little things which, after you have graduated to the ranks of the experienced motoriste, you will buy, not because they are absolutely necessary, but because of their convenience. For instance, a speedometer. All the half-dozen makes are good ones. A speedometer is a very interesting accessory, for it tells you exactly the pace at which you are travelling, and in some instances has been known to influence the decision of a magistrate when deciding a charge of exceeding the speed-limit. (1909)

Carry a Weapon

If you are going to drive alone on the highways and byways it might be advisable to carry a small revolver. I have an automatic "Colt," and find it very easy to handle as there is practically no recoil — a great consideration to a woman. While I have never had occasion to use it on the road (though, I may add, I practise continually at a range to keep my eye and hand "in") it is nevertheless a comfort to know that should the occasion arise I have the means of defending myself. (1909)

"Be sure you are right, then go ahead." This good old motto is just the thing to remember when one is going in for motoring. (1909)

MUSIC.

1870

Music, a protection against vice, an incentive to virture. (1882)

A Song Instead of a Speech

OTHING enlivens a dinner-party more than an occasional song, especially when the company is so well warmed with wine as to become a little impatient at the restraints necessarily imposed in listening to speeches. (1860)

A Musical Quiz

In what key would a lover compose a proposal of marriage? Answer: In the key of be mine, ah! (*Frank Leslie's Pleasant Hours*, 1885)

Hold Your Tongue

Nothing is more rude than to converse whilst people are singing. If you do not like music sufficiently to listen to it, you should remember that others may do so, and that not only do you interrupt their enjoyment of it, but you offer an offence to the singers. (1868)

1882

Music as Bait

Girls are taught music almost as a matter of course, and too often merely consider it as a bait to lure a lover. The lover being lured, the bait is detached from the hook, and looked upon as useless for the rest of existence. (1868)

Don't Mangle Your Song

If you are invited to sing, accept at once. Do not hurry up to the piano, as if glad of an opportunity to show off, but go gently. If, by request, you have brought your music, leave it down stairs; it can be sent for. In the choice of songs, variety is to be adopted. German music pleases generally; but let no one not conversant with the right pronunciation of any foreign language sing in it; there is nothing so unpleasant as broad French, mincing German, or lisping Italian. (1868)

> *One singer said to another, "my daughter inherited my voice." "Oh," said the other with the most innocent air. "That is the explanation then. I have always wondered where it was."*
> **(Frank Leslie's Pleasant Hours, 1885)**

Never, Never, Never

- Never laugh at the misfortunes of others.
- Never give a promise that you do not fulfill.
- Never send a present, hoping for one in return.
- Never fail to be punctual at the time appointed.
- Never make yourself the hero of your own story.
- Never fail to give a polite answer to a civil question.
- Never question a servant or a child about family matters.
- Never read letters which you may find addressed to others.
- Never refer to a gift you have made, or favor you have rendered.
- Never neglect to call upon your friends.
- Never look over the shoulder of another who is reading.
- Never appear to notice a scar, deformity, or defect of anyone present.
- Never punish your child for a fault to which you are addicted yourself.
- Never lend an article you have borrowed, unless you have permission to do so.
- Never attempt to draw the attention of the company constantly upon yourself.
- Never exhibit anger, impatience or excitement, when an accident happens.
  (1883)

1877

Never, Never, Never

- Never enter a room noisily; never fail to close the door after you, and never slam it.
- Never refuse to receive an apology.
- Never exaggerate.
- Never exhibit too great familiarity with the new acquaintance.
- Never fail to tell the truth. If truthful, you get your reward.
- Never enter a room filled with people, without a slight bow to the general company when first entering.
- Never speak much of your own performances.
- Never point at another.
- Never wantonly frighten others.
- Never borrow money and neglect to pay. If you do, you will soon be known as a person of no business integrity.
- Never betray a confidence.
- Never leave home with unkind words.
- Never fail to offer the easiest and best seat in the room to an invalid, an elderly person, or a lady.
- Never fail to say kind and encouraging words to those whom you meet in distress. Your kindness may lift them out of their despair.
- Never will a gentleman allude to conquests which he may have made with ladies.
- Never send your guest, who is accustomed to a warm room, off into a cold, damp, spare bed, to sleep.
- Never write to another asking for information, or a favor of any kind, without enclosing a postage stamp for the reply.
- Never attempt to convey the impression that you are a genius.
- Never call attention to the features or form of anyone present.
- Never present a gift saying that it is of no use to yourself.
- Never associate with bad company.
- Never cross the leg and put out one foot in the street-car, or places where it will trouble others when passing by. (1883)

Calling with a Dog

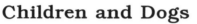

NO dog, however "dear or interesting," can be admitted to the drawing-room, and it is bad taste to have one follow you from home, if you intend to make calls. (1869)

Children and Dogs

Never allow young children, dogs or pets of any sort to accompany you in a call. They often prove disagreeable and troublesome. (1882)

1878

On a Train

Passengers should not carry anything on the train that would be offensive to others. They should most rigidly avoid boarding the train with dogs of any kind, whether spaniels, pointers, or poodles. (1899)

1889

Social Justice

A rich murderer might get off scot free but if a poor wretch steals a loaf of bread for his starving family, the zeal and fury of the police know no bounds, and the fellow is lucky if he is not brained on the spot. (*Harper's Weekly*, 1859)

Native Ground
Books & Music

1883

The Dram-Shop

It is not surprising that people who are compelled to live in tenements unfit for horses, or even swine, resort to the dram-shop when the work of the day is over, and try to hide their wretchedness from themselves in the convivialities of a well-lighted saloon and the delirium of intoxication...Health and morals require something more than soup and sentiment. (*New York Graphic*, 1874)

Women as Bread-Winners

It is a defect of our civilization that women are forced to become bread-winners. Young girls who ought to be training in the school at home for the high and holy duties of wifehood and motherhood are compelled by social and industrial maladjustments to enter the hurly-burly of the great work-a-day world, competing with those who ought to support them in the desperate struggle for existence, every year, it seems, growing more fierce. (1892)

1897

"No man in this land suffers from poverty, unless it be more than his fault — unless it be his sin." Henry Ward Beecher, 1875

How Should Poor Folk Live?

An unpleasant subject, is it? Possibly it may be. It is none the less one of thrilling interest and unquenchable importance. We may crowd it into a corner and bid it stay out of sight. No sooner have we packed it snugly away, than it begins to lift its unlovely head and to distribute unsavory odors. Exactly what to do with the poor people of the great cities has always been one of the most difficult of social questions. Where they shall be put, how they shall be lodged, on what they shall be fed, wherewithal they shall be clothed, and in what manner education and religion and justice shall be dealt out to them — these are knotty questions. Philosophers have wrestled with these; moralists have essayed to solve them; theologians have preached on them; politicians have made capital of them; and charlatans have tinkered with them. In poverty itself there is no crime. (*Frank Leslie's Sunday Magazine*, 1881)

Proposals of Marriage

Dishevelled Proposals

NO girl wants to be proposed to when her hair is dishevelled, her collar wilted, and her soul distraught by pestiferous mosquitoes. (1901)

In His Hands

Since the customs of society have awarded to men the privilege of making the first advance toward matrimony, it is the safest and happiest way for women to leave the matter entirely in his hands. (1838)

Men Propose Thoughtlessly

After the first few times, men propose as thoughtlessly and easily as they dress for dinner, that they devote no particular study to the art, that constant practice makes them proficient, and that almost any girl will do when the proposal mood is on. (1901)

Nothing strengthens a woman's self-confidence like a proposal. (1901)

Moonlight Proposals

No wise girl would accept a man who proposed by moonlight or just after a meal. The dear things are n't themselves then. Food, properly served, will attract a proposal at almost any time, especially if it is known that the pleasing viands were of the girl's own making. (1901)

Sincere Proposals

It is very hard to tell whether a man really means a proposal. It may have been made under romantic circumstances, or because he was lonesome for the other girl, or, in the case of an heiress, because he was tired of work. Longing for the absent sweetheart will frequently cause a man to become engaged to someone near by, because, though absence may make a woman's heart grow fonder, it is presence that plays the mischief with a man. (1901)

Don't Be Afraid

Given a pair of hands, a brave heart, and a small salary, a young man should not be afraid to ask a sensible girl to share his lot. (1910)

Written Proposals

A written proposal is extremely bad form. A girl never can be sure that her lover did not attempt to fish it out of the letter-box after it had slipped from his fingers. (1901)

Proposals of Marriage

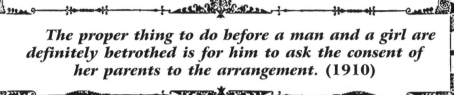

The proper thing to do before a man and a girl are definitely betrothed is for him to ask the consent of her parents to the arrangement. **(1910)**

Asking Papa

The proposal over and the lady's acceptance secured, the next thing is to "see papa." And here is an ordeal that will test the courage of the boldest lover. The old folks will not be looking at your suit from the sentimental side. They will take the practical view, and it will behoove you, therefore, to bear this fact in mind. If you shift from one foot to the other, fidgeting a good deal, and giving your hat a closer inspection than it ever had before, while your heart thumps like a trip-hammer, and your tongue becomes unmanageable, console yourself, if you can, with the reflection that the stern father who now confronts you so coolly, and it may be with such an air of superiority, has himself faced a like ordeal; and then plunge desperately into the midst of your subject. You may not be very coherent, and possibly you will be quite ridiculous, but the old folks will understand, and make all necessary allowances. You will have been eloquent and explicit enough if you have simply said, "Can Mary be my wife?" (1892)

Proposals of Marriage

Asking For Her Hand

A spoken declaration should be bold, manly and earnest, and so plain in its meaning that there can be no misunderstanding. As to the exact words to be used, there can be no set formula; each proposer must be governed by his own ideas and sense of propriety in the matter. (1882)

1912

A Lady's First Refusal

It is not always necessary to take a lady's first refusal as absolute. Diffidence or uncertainty as to her own feelings may sometimes influence a lady to reply in the negative, and after consideration cause her to regret that reply. (1882)

The Greatest Compliment

The offer of a man's heart and hand, is the greatest compliment he can pay you, however undesirable to you these gifts may be. (1838)

Etiquette Quiz

Should a man who has been accepted by a young lady, ask her father's consent, if he has no intention of marrying immediately?

Yes, he should ask the parents' consent at once, and frankly state his financial condition and future prospects. (1889)

Just Say "No"

No lady worthy any gentleman's regard will say "no" twice to a suit which she intends ultimately to receive with favor. (1882)

Refusing an Offer of Marriage

In refusing, the lady ought to convey her full sense of the high honor intended her by the gentleman, and to add, seriously but not offensively, that it is not in accordance with her inclination, or that circumstances compel her to give an unfavorable answer. (1882)

1899

Don't Keep Him in Suspense

A woman of considerate feelings will not keep a lover in suspense. When she sees clearly that she has become the object of his especial regard, and she does not wish to encourage his addresses, she will take the earliest opportunity offering to make known the state of her mind. She will not be harsh, but generous and humane. (1892)

Marrying on Nothing

A man should not court a girl, nor ask her to become his fiancee unless he is reasonably sure he can support a wife. To marry on nothing at all is very foolish, and seldom results happily. (1910)

1877

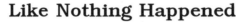

Like Nothing Happened

F you are so situated as to meet the gentleman whose hand you have refused, you should do it with frank cordiality, and put him at ease by behaving as if nothing particular had passed between you.

Unmanly Conduct

Rejected suitors sometimes act as if they had received injuries they were bound to avenge, and so take every opportunity of annoying or slighting the helpless victims of their former attentions. Such conduct is cowardly and unmanly, to say nothing of its utter violation of good breeding. (1894)

1883

Always endeavor to make true friends of your rejected lover. (1838)

Mistaken Tenderness

Inexperienced girls sometimes feel so much the pain they are inflicting, that they use phrases which feed a lover's hopes; but this is mistaken tenderness; your answer should be as decided, as it is courteous. (1838)

Unladylike Conduct Toward a Suitor

It is only the contemptible flirt that keeps an honorable man in suspense for the purpose of glorifying herself by his attentions in the eyes of friends. Nor would any but a frivolous or vicious girl boast of the offer she had received and rejected. Such an offer is a privileged communication. The secret of it should be held sacred. No true lady will ever divulge to anyone, unless it may be to her mother, the fact of such an offer. It is the severest breach of honor to do so. (1882)

Giving Back the Engagement Ring

1880

Duty of a Rejected Suitor

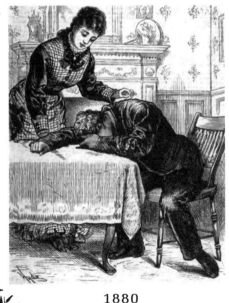

1880

The duty of the rejected suitor is quite clear. Etiquette demands that he shall accept the lady's decision as final and retire from the field. He has no right to demand the reason of her refusal. If she assign it, he is bound to respect her secret, if it is one, and to hold it inviolable. To persist in urging his suit or to follow up the lady with marked attentions would be in the worst possible taste. The proper course is to withdraw as much as possible from the circles in which she moves, so that she may be spared reminiscences which can not be other than painful. (1894)

Rejected Lovers

1878

The Rejected Lover

If a gentleman makes a lady an offer, she has no right to speak of it. If she possess either generosity or gratitude for offered affection, she will not betray a secret which does not belong to her. It is sufficiently painful to be refused, without incurring the additional mortification of being pointed out as a rejected lover. (1894)

Breaking an Engagement

It sometimes becomes necessary to break off an engagement. If anything is developed that will make the marriage unhappy, it is far better to break it off than otherwise. Always break an engagement by letter. In this way the reasons can be set forth fully without the embarrassment of the other's presence. Upon the dissolution of an engagement all letters, pictures, presents, etc., received should be returned. (1893)

Acknowledging Such Letter

Such a letter should be acknowledged in a dignified manner, and no efforts should be made or measures be taken to change the decision of the writer unless it is manifest that he or she is greatly mistaken in his or her premises. A similar return of letters, portraits and gifts should be made. (1881)

1886

Parents: Guard Your Daughters from the *temptations of rural life*. (1910)

The Lurking Serpent of Rural Bliss

1879

HE sweet green country, with its homes nestled among the trees, its lovely leafy lanes, its fragrant summer twilight, and its sequestered and cloistered quietude, is not a paradise unmolested by the serpent. Into that Eden he too often glides, and in that Eden he too often lurks, uplifting his haughty crest, and sticking out his forked tongue and inserting his poisonous fangs. (1910)

God made the country and man made the town. (*Herald of Health,* 1871)

Evil creeps in when folly leaves a gap in the hedge. (1910)

City life has advantages — gas for light, and water on all the floors of the house, shops close at hand, the butcher, the baker, the carpenter, the grocer, the tailor, and the haberdasher within easy call. (*Herald of Health*, 1871)

1877

In the country, privacy is the
handmaid of temptation. (1910)

Advice to The New Master

The first thing you need is courage; do not let the boys think that you are afraid. Do not come into the room with your eyes cast down, but look the form in the face. Great is the influence of a steady eye. We have all of us known some quiet, strong-nerved man whose gaze had a strange power over untamed animals, and you want to gain the same kind of influence over untamed boys. (1905b)

Dos & Don'ts For The New Master

1. Never lose your head or your temper.
2. Make up your mind beforehand exactly what you will and what you will not allow.
3. Make it perfectly clear to the form what your standard is.
4. Always appear to take for granted that you will get what you want.
5. Having said what you will do, do not change your mind if it can possibly be avoided.
6. Never let a boy off from kindness of heart.
7. Never threaten vaguely or indulge in general declamations.
8. Do not grumble or implore.
9. Do not be always nagging.
10. Never let a boy argue about his punishment. (1905b)

Punishment

All punishment is a confession of weakness, for it shows that the moral influence of the school and master has proved insufficient to prevent the commission of the offence. (1905b)

Make an Impression

Your punishment must be severe enough to make the desired impression. If you cane, cane hard; if you keep in, keep in long enough. If a boy has something to write, see that it is written really well; if you give him something to learn, do not let him go until he has said it perfectly. Make it a rule to which there can be no exceptions that slovenly punishments are never taken. (1905b)

Authority Must Rest on FEAR

In the beginning you must base your authority on fear. There is no getting over the fact that a new master will, as a rule, be promptly obeyed only if he inspires a wholesome dread of what he will do in cases of disobedience. (1905b)

1899

Politeness at School

It is not polite to frown or sulk or "answer back," when you are reproved for some neglect or offence. It is not polite to complain of the quality or the quantity of the food which is set before you. (1900)

Salute Your Teacher

Always salute your teacher distinctly when you enter the schoolroom. Do the same to your class-mates, even if it be only with a bow or a smile. A well-bred scholar will give the teacher as little trouble as possible. (1900)

The Harsh Teacher

If your teacher seems to be harsh or partial, do not take it for granted that he is so; possibly you are mistaken. Wait a while. If there are brighter scholars in the class than you, be proud of them, praise them; do not dislike them; try by all fair means to excel them. (1900)

1899

The Three "R's"

The illiterate population sends eight times its quota to jails and prison as the literate population. (*Harper's New Monthly Magazine,* 1894)

Watch Your Tone

A high and loud tone of voice should not have place in a schoolroom. (1888)

Why did Adam bite the apple? said a school-master to a country lad. "'Cause he had no knife," said the urchin.
(Frank Leslie's Pleasant Hours, 1885)

Playing Hooky

The bad boy of school age has no comfort at all if his city has adopted the Attendance Law. Let him try a ride on a freight-car, or a quiet game of craps, or the cool delights of an ice-wagon with its frozen chunks that turn one's throat to marble. Relentless as fate, the truant officer appears on his trail. Escape is hopeless. (*The Century*, 1903)

For Company Only

Young people sometimes seem to think good manners are to be put on as fine clothes are, not for every-day wear, but for company only. (1888)

The Kindergarten

Into the slums of the cities flock the three classes of weaklings — the unthrifty, the criminal, and the inebriates. The kindergarten can do much to stop the increase of the slum classes by educating their children in the tender years when their education is possible. (*Harper's New Monthly Magazine,* 1894)

1912

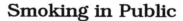

Smoking in Public

ONE may never smoke in the company of the fair. One must never smoke in the streets, that is, in daylight. The deadly crime may be committed, like burglary, after dark, but not before. One must never smoke in a closed carriage. Besides being coarse and atrocious, smoking is very bad for the health. (1875)

Smoking and the Clergy

One must never smoke, without consent, in the presence of a clergyman, and one must never offer a cigar to any ecclesiastic. (1875)

The Smoking Animal

The tobacco smoker, in public, is the most selfish animal imaginable; he perseveres in contaminating the pure and fragrant air, careless whom he annoys, and is but the fitting inmate of a tavern. (1843)

In a Railway Car

One may smoke in a railway-carriage in spite of by-laws, if one first obtains the consent of every one present, but if there is a lady there, though she has given her consent, smoke not. (1875)

Civilized Behavior

If you are so unfortunate as to have contracted the low habit of smoking, be careful to practice it under certain restrictions; at least, so long as you are desirous of being considered fit for civilized society. (1843)

Smoking Clothes

If you smoke, and you are to wear your clothes in the presence of ladies afterward, you must change them to smoke in. (1875)

Smokers & Chewers

> *Tobacco is confessedly one of the most virulent poisons in nature.* **(1875)**

1880

Ladies Who Smoke

If a woman has true regard for herself, she should not indulge in smoking; if she does, it should be in absolute privacy. (1904)

Snuff Takers

You have seen a man who took snuff copiously, and who generally had his breast covered with snuff, abandon this vile habit. (1894)

The Bachelor's Wife

The pipe is the bachelor's wife. With it, he can endure solitude longer, and is not forced into low society in order to shun it. With it, the idle can pass many an hour, which otherwise he would have given, not to work, but to extravagant devilries. With it, he is no longer restless and impatient for excitement of any kind. I foresee with dread a too tender allegiance to the pipe, to the destruction of good society, and the abandonment of the

1883

ladies. It's no wonder they hate it, dear creatures; the pipe is the worst rival a woman can have. And it is one whose eyes she cannot scratch out, who improves with age, while she herself declines. (1875)

Changing Times

At one time it was considered a sign of infamously bad taste to smoke in the presence of women in any circumstances. But it is now no longer so. So many women smoke themselves, that in some houses even the drawing-room is thrown open to Princess Nicotine. (1897)

1879

A lady's assurance that she does not object to the odor of a cigar may be accepted by a gentleman as permission to continue smoking. (1889d)

Your Dear Wife

If your wife dislikes cigars — and few young women like to have their clothes tainted by tobacco — leave off smoking; for it is at best, an ungentlemanly and dirty habit. (1894)

"Doctor, said an old gentleman who was an inveterate snuff-taker, to a physician, "is it true that snuff destroys the olfactory nerves, clogs and otherwise destroys the brain?" "It cannot be true," came the caustic reply, "since those who have any brains never take snuff at all." (1843)

Spinsterhood

IT may truly be said that a real man, a good, square, honest, God-loving man, would never be guilty of asking a young untried, undeveloped girl to assume such tremendous responsibilities. The man who does is simply a monster of selfishness, and that is enough to know about any man. So girls, don't look in such directions for a way out of spinsterhood. If you do you will forever regret it, and will be obliged to work out your mistakes through the hardest and most crucifying experience. (*The Ladies World*, June, 1897)

1912

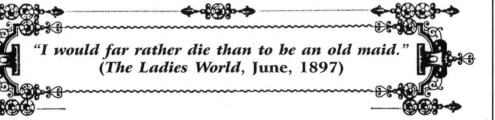

"I would far rather die than to be an old maid."
(**The Ladies World**, June, 1897)

A Forlorn Spinster

Let parents teach their daughters and let girls understand for themselves that happiness, or peace, in married life is impossible where a man is, in any wise, dissipated, or liable to be overcome by any of the fashionable vices of the day. Better go down to your grave a "forlorn spinster" than marry such a man. (1896b)

Giving Up Your Seat

THE old custom of a man giving up his seat in a street-car to a woman is being gradually done away with. This is due largely to the fact that women are now so extensively engaged in commercial business that they are constant riders at the busy hours, and thus come into direct competition with men. A well-bred man, however, will show his manliness by giving any woman his seat and standing himself, as she is less fitted for such hardships and annoyances. (1904)

A Man's Duty

It is good form for a man to assist a woman getting on or off a car. If a man is accompanied by a woman when she leaves the car, he should help her off the car. A man should always be polite and courteous toward a conductor, as the latter's position is a hard and trying one. A man should never cross his legs or keep his feet extended in the passageway. If a man finds it necessary to crowd into a car already full, he should do so with consideration and politeness, and with an apology for pressing against any one. (1904)

A Pained Air

A woman should not look with a pained and injured air at the men passengers because no one of them has offered her a seat. (1904)

Standard Equipment

Street cars are equipped with all modern conveniences, including hot and cold conductors and running transfers, this modern octopus rules the great highways of our teeming cities with an iron hand and a steal franchise. (1906b)

Seats for Ladies

Gentlemen formerly rose and offered seats to ladies in street cars. This practice has fallen into desuetude now for several excellent reasons. One is the increasing independence of women who compete with men on equal terms in every industrial field, and who, in becoming equals, and competitors, cease to be superiors and, so to speak, royalty. Another is the extreme rudeness of women who accept preferred seats without the slightest inclination of the head, or the very faintest word of thanks. (1910)

1912

THE gentleman should bow to every lady he knows, without waiting for her recognition. If the gentleman be smoking, he must remove his cigar from his mouth while bowing to the lady. (1892)

A gentleman always throws away his cigar when he turns to walk with ladies. (1910)

A gentleman is always polite, in the parlor, dining-room, or on the street. A man who will annoy or insult a lady in the street, lowers himself to a brute, no matter whether he offends by look, word or gesture. (1875)

When you are escorting a lady in the street, politeness does not absolutely require you carry her bundle or parasol, but if you are gallant, you will do so. You must regulate your walk to hers, and not force her to keep up with your ordinary pace. (1875)

When a lady is crossing a muddy street she should gather her dress in her right hand, and draw it to her right side. (1910)

Gentlemen lift their hats when passing ladies who are strangers on staircases, in corridors, in elevators, and entering public rooms. (1910)

It is rude to stare at ladies in the street. (1910)

1883

In a crowd, never rudely push aside those who impede your progress, but wait patiently until the way is clear. If you are hurried by business of importance or an engagement, you will find that a few courteous words will open the way before you more quickly than the most violent pushing and loud talking. (1875)

1880

Be careful walking with or near a lady, not to put your foot upon her dress. (1875)

Don't eat fruit, or anything else on the public streets. A gentleman on the promenade, engaged in munching an apple or a pear, presents a more amusing than edifying picture. (1884)

In walking with a lady, the gentleman should keep next to the carriage-way. (1860)

Street Etiquette

Crossing a Muddy Street

When tripping over the pavement, a lady should gracefully raise her dress a little above her ankle. With her right hand she should hold together the folds of her gown and draw them toward the right side. To raise the dress on both sides, and with both hands, is vulgar. This ungraceful practice can be tolerated only for a moment when the mud is very deep. (1881)

Smoking on the Street

Do not smoke on the street until after dark, and then remove your cigar from your mouth, if you meet a lady. (1875)

Street Attire

Be careful about your dress. You can never know whom you may meet, so it is best to never leave the house other-wise than well-dressed. (1875)

Put on Your Hat!

On a cold day when a man stands talking with a woman with his head uncovered, she should say, "Pray, put on your hat! I'm afraid you will catch cold." (1905)

Walking with an Umbrella

In carrying an umbrella, avoid striking your umbrella against those which pass you; if you are walking with a lady, let the umbrella cover her perfectly, but hold it so that you will not touch her bonnet. (1875)

1906

No Monkey Business

Whether young or old, they will form no acquaintances on the streets, and their conduct will be marked by a modest reserve, which will keep impertinence at a distance, and disarm criticism. The very appearance of evil must be avoided, and she is not a true lady who so carries herself in the public thoroughfare that loafers stare as she goes by and "mashers" follow her with insulting attentions. (1892)

1883

Walking Alone

When a gentleman is walking alone, he must always turn aside to give the upper side of the pavement to a lady, to any one carrying a heavy load, to a clergyman, or to an old gentleman. (1869)

Flippant Step of a Dandy

It is a great thing to be able to walk like a gentleman — that is, to get rid of the awkward, lounging, swinging gait of a clown, and stop before you reach the affected and flippant step of a dandy. (1860)

Etiquette Quiz

In crossing a narrow or a slippery plank, who should go first, the lady or the gentleman?

The lady should go first, with the gentleman following close behind, to aid her if required.

Eat Slowly

ID you not hear that Napoleon lost the battle of Leipzig by eating too fast? It is a fact though. His haste caused indigestion, which made him incapable of attending to the details of the battle. (1875)

Common Blunders to Avoid

- Do not eat fast.
- Do not make noise with mouth or throat.
- Do not fill the mouth too full.
- Do not open the mouth in masticating.
- Do not leave the table with food in your mouth.
- Be careful to avoid soiling the cloth.
- Do not cut your bread; break it.
- Never carry any part of the food with you from the table.
- Never apologize to the waitress for making trouble; it is her business to serve you, but treat her with courtesy.
- Do not pick your teeth or put your fingers in your mouth at the table.
- Do not refuse to take the last piece of bread or cake. (1910)

1857

Table Manners

1877

Do not trifle with your knife or fork, or drum on the table, or fidget in any way, while waiting to be served. (1910)

You must not bury your face in your plate; you came to show it, and it ought to be alive. (1860)

Never pile food on your plate like you are starving, but take a little at a time; the dishes will not run away. (1875)

Accustom yourself to eat with the left hand, thus avoiding the necessity of shifting the fork from one hand to the other. (1892)

Don't Wait

As soon as you are helped at the table, begin to eat. It is old-fashioned and ill-bred to wait for others. If the food is too hot to begin eating of it at once, take up the knife and fork and appear to begin. (1892)

Manners Eating Soup

Never blow your soup if it is too hot, but wait until it cools. Never raise your plate to your lips, but eat with your spoon. Never take soup twice. (1875)

Only to gentlemen possessed of a luxuriant mustache is it permitted to take soup from the point of the spoon, always providing they can do so skillfully and without an awkward use of the arm. (1896b)

I have seen men who eat soup or chewed their food, in so noisy a manner, as to be heard from one end of the table to the other; fill their mouths so full of food, that they threaten suffocation or choking; use their own knife for the butter, and salt; put fingers in the sugar bowl, and commit other faults quite as monstrous, yet seem to be perfectly unconscious that they were doing anything to attract attention. (1875)

I beg you will not make that odious noise in drinking your soup. It is louder than a dog lapping water. (1875)

Using Your Knife

Never use your knife for any purpose but to cut your food. It is not meant to put food in your mouth. Your fork is intended to carry food from your plate to your mouth, and no gentleman ever eats with his knife. (1875)

1879

Table Manners

1877

Unmentionables on Your Plate

If in the leaves of your salad or in a plate of fruit you find a worm or insect, pass your plate to the waiter, without any comment, and he will bring you another. (1875)

Be careful to avoid the extremes of gluttony or over daintiness at the table. To eat enormously is disgusting; but if you eat too sparingly, your host may think you despise his fare. (1875)

Forks were, undoubtedly, a later invention than fingers, but as we are not cannibals, I am inclined to think they are a good one. (1875)

A guest should never find fault with the dinner or with any part of it. (1881)

Table Manners

1899

Guarding Your Plate

Some people, in military style, in the intervals of cramming, makes his knife and fork keep guard over the jealously watched plate, being held upright of either side, with clenched fist, like the musket of a raw recruit. (1875)

Feeding Time

Chomp, chomp; smack, smack, — it is one thing to know how to make a pudding, and another to know how to eat it when made. Unmerciful and monstrous are the noises with which some persons accompany the eating — no, the devouring of the food for which, we trust, they are thankful. To sit down with a company of such masticators is like joining a herd of swine feeding. Some persons gnaw on a crust of bread as dogs gnaw a bone. (1875)

Etiquette Quiz
What should you do if a fly falls in your coffee?

Do not mention the fact, but silently send your cup away to be refilled. (1892)

Table Manners

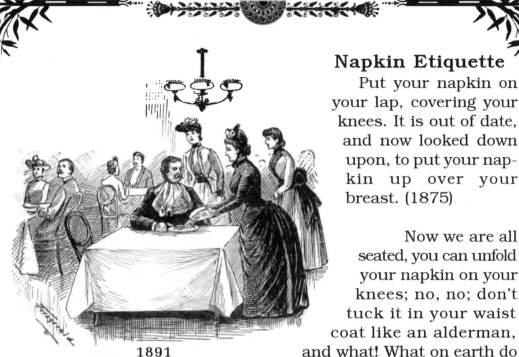

1891

Napkin Etiquette

Put your napkin on your lap, covering your knees. It is out of date, and now looked down upon, to put your napkin up over your breast. (1875)

Now we are all seated, you can unfold your napkin on your knees; no, no; don't tuck it in your waist coat like an alderman, and what! What on earth do you mean by wiping your forehead with it? Do you take it for a towel? Well, never mind, I am consoled that you did not go further, and use it as a pocket-handkerchief. (1875)

In the event you want to cough or sneeze, leave the table, if possible. If not, lean back and turn your head. A sneeze, it is said, may be suppressed by placing the finger firmly upon the upper lip. (1892)

Always use the salt-spoon, sugar-tongs or butter-knife; to use your own knife, spoon, or fingers, evinces a shocking want of good-breeding. (1875)

Never dip a piece of bread in gravy or preserves upon your plate and then bite it, but if you wish to eat them together, break the bread into small pieces and carry those to your mouth with your fork. (1875)

1891

Sensible Table Manners

- Do not play with the table utensils, or crumble the bread.
- Do not put your elbows on the table, or sit too far back, or lounge.
- Do not talk loud or boisterously.
- Be cheerful in conduct and conversation.
- Never, if possible, cough or sneeze at the table.
- Do not bend the head low down over the plate. The food should go to the mouth, not the mouth to the food.
- Never tilt back your chair while at table, or at any other time.
- Never make a noise while eating.
- Do not open the mouth while chewing, but keep the lips closed.

1897

- Do not talk when the mouth is full.
- Never put fruit or bon-bons in your pocket to carry them from the table.
- It is not necessary to show persons how you masticate your food.
- When you are at the table do not show restlessness, by fidgeting in your seat, or moving the feet about unnecessarily. (1875)
- Do not introduce disgusting or unpleasant topics of conversation. (1910)

1880

Table Manners

Bad Table Manners

1. Tips chair back.
2. Eats with his mouth too full.
3. Feeds a dog at the table.
4. Holds his knife improperly.
5. Engages in arguments at mealtime.
6. Lounges on the table.
7. Brings a cross child to the table.
8. Drinks from a saucer and laps the last drop.
9. Comes to the table in shirt sleeves, and puts his feet beside the chair.
10. Picks his teeth with his fingers.
11. Scratches her head and gets up unnecessarily. (1883)

Etiquette Quiz
Is it allowable for a man to eat his meals with his coat off?

Certainly not. No well-bred man would think of doing so. (1889)

Telephone Etiquette

Women and the Telephone

THE American woman is becoming dependent upon the telephone. She orders the family dinner by telephone, upbraids her dressmaker by telephone and electioneers by telephone for the presidency of her club.

If she happens to live in a house equipped with the latest pattern of telephone apparatus, she gives orders to the cook in the kitchen without leaving her chair, for the telephone has taken the place of the speaking-tube in the up-to-date city residence. No habit grows more rapidly than the telephone habit. (*New Era Illustrated Magazine,* 1904)

Social Equals

Messages should be sent only to social equals. (*New Era Illustrated Magazine*, 1904)

Telephone Invitations

Telephone invitations should be sent only to those with whom the utmost intimacy exists, and who will pardon the informality. (1904)

A Necessity

The telephone is now so much used to give invitations among intimate friends, and especially by young people, that it has become a social necessity. (1912)

1896

A Date to Remember

ONDAY, December 21, 1874, is remembered as the day upon which occurred the first surrender ever made by a liquor-dealer of his stock of liquors to the women in answer to their prayers and by them poured into the street. Nearly a thousand men, women and children witnessed the mingling of beer, ale, wine and whisky, as they filled the gutters, and were drunk up by the earth, while bells were ringing, men and boys shouting, and women praying to God, who had given the victory. In eight days all the eleven saloons had been closed, and the three drug-stores were pledged to sell only by prescription. (*Frank Leslie's Sunday Magazine*, 1881)

Washington, Ohio, December 1874

First and Last

B E the last to enter the carriage, the first to leave it. If you have ladies with you, offer your hand to assist them in entering and alighting and you should take the arm of an old gentleman to assist him. (1865)

1896

Assisting a Lady

If you see a lady leaving a carriage unattended, or hesitating at a bad crossing, you may, with propriety, offer your hand or arm to assist her, and having seen her safely upon the pavement, bow and pass on. (1865)

Learning to Drive

To learn to drive requires time and patience. Study the methods of a good coachman. A woman should understand the methods of harnessing a horse, and before starting on a journey it is important to know that every bit of the harness, the reins, and everything connected to the gear, are just as they should be. (1910)

Offering Your Arm

When the ladies get off the coach, offer them your arm, and do the same when the coachman is driving rapidly over a rough place. (1836)

Brutes and Knaves

It is an extremely difficult affair to travel in a coach with perfect propriety. Ten to one the person next to you is an English nobleman incognito; and a hundred to one, the man opposite you is a brute or a knave. To behave so that you may not be uncivil to the one, nor a dupe to the other, is an art of some niceness. (1836)

Never Say "Yes"

When the owner of a wagon is driving a gentleman, it is courteous to offer the reins, but the offer should always be declined. (1892)

Leaving a Carriage

Learn how to leave and enter a carriage gracefully. Some people merely tumble out and in. To get into a carriage gracefully is a necessary art, and should be performed without either loitering or haste. (1910)

One Horse

In learning to drive, start with one horse. The first lesson is to hold the reins properly and to sit in a good position in the driving-seat. The left hand and wrist should be held straight, not stiffly, but naturally; the little finger down, the thumb and first finger uppermost. The elbows should be close to the body. (1910)

Travel by Coach or Carriage

Entering a Carriage

If you enter a carriage with a lady, let her first take her place on the seat facing the horses; then sit opposite, and on no account beside her, unless you are her husband or other near relative. Enter a carriage so that your back is towards the seat you are to occupy; you will thus avoid turning round in the carriage, which is awkward. Take care that you do not trample on the ladies' dresses, or shut them in as you close the door. (1883)

Alighting From a Carriage

The rule in all cases is this: You quit the carriage first and hand the lady out. (1881)

Tipping the Coachman

It is customary when a guest leaves a house party after a visit to give the coachman a tip. (1904)

Sleeping in a Carriage

Take care not to lean upon the shoulder of your neighbor when you sleep. (1836)

1879

Seat of Honor

In a carriage, where a coachman is outside, the seat of honor is that on the right hand, facing the horses. It is accorded the lady, an elderly person, or the guest. (1892)

Impertinent Rudeness

A gentleman must not put his arm across the back of the seat when driving with a lady. To do so is an extreme case of impertinent rudeness. (1892)

Carriage Etiquette

It is quite an art to enter or leave a carriage gracefully, and gentlemen cannot be too careful of what they do. To trample a lady's dress, or shut her shawl in the door is extremely awkward. (1892)

Etiquette Quiz

When a lady and gentleman are traveling together, which should leave the carriage first?

The gentleman, to help her out. (1889)

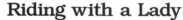

Riding with a Lady

I N attending a lady in a horse-back ride, never mount your horse until she is ready to start. Give her your hand to assist her in mounting, arrange the folds of her habit, hand her her reins and her whip, and then take your own seat in

1883

your saddle. Before permitting the lady to mount, her escort must carefully examine the girths and stirrups of her saddle, and the bit and reins of the bridle. Not a strap or buckle should escape inspection, and every possible precaution should be taken against accident. (1892)

If the road is muddy, be careful that you do not ride so as to bespatter her habit. (1875)

The gentleman must pay all tolls, and when a fence or ditch is to be cleared he must leap first. (1892)

Dressing for the Ride

The correct dress for men is full riding-breeches, close-fitting at the knee, leggings, a high-buttoned waistcoat, and a coat with the conventional short cutaway tails. The hat is an alpine or a derby, and the tie the regulation stock. These, with riding-gloves and a riding-crop, constitute the regular riding-dress for a young man. A man should always consult his tailor, that the dress in all its details may be strictly up to date. (1904)

Riding Dress for Women

There is a well-prescribed riding-dress for women as for men. The habit of dark material, with skirt falling just over the feet when in the saddle, and the close-fitting waist, with long or short tails, together with the white collar and black or white tie, constitute the regulation dress. The derby hat is smaller than formerly. Gloves of a dark color and a crop with a bone handle are always in place.

1889

Any jewelry, save that which is absolutely necessary, should be shunned. As in the case of a man, a woman should consult a tailor of good practical experience, that her costume may be in the correct style. (1904)

Throwing Dust

If you travel on horseback, in distinguished company, and happen to be on the windward side, so that you throw dust upon your companion, you should change your position. When we pass by trees the branches of which are about the height of our shoulders, the one who goes first ought to take care that the branches, in going back to their former situation, should not strike with violence against the person who follows. (1841)

Dismounting

In dismounting, a gentleman offers a lady his right hand, taking her left. His own left hand he uses as a step for her foot, declining it gently as soon as she rises from the saddle. (1892)

Pace in Riding

The lady must always decide upon the pace. It is ungenerous to urge her or incite her horse to a faster gait than she feels competent to undertake. Keep to the right of the lady or ladies riding with you. Open all gates and pay all tolls on the road. (1881)

1890

Spoiling Your Horse

One must remember that in riding it is essential to be on good terms with one's horse. A person who forgets this and loses self-control is almost certain to be a bad rider, and to spoil his horse. (1910)

1877

1880

Fording a Body of Water

If you are fording a large stream, a small river, or a muddy pool, it is polite to go first; but if you have not taken this precaution, and fall in the rear, you ought to keep at a distance, so that the horse's feet may not spatter the water or mud upon the gentleman before you. If your companion gallops his horse, you should never pass him, nor make your horse caper, unless he signifies that it is agreeable to him. (1841)

Riding with an Elderly Gentleman

In riding with an elderly gentleman, a younger man should extend all the courtesies of the road, the shady side, the choice of speed, the choice also of direction, and, if there be a difference, the best horse. (1869)

The Kindly Ticket Agent

HE ticket agent should have a kind word for every one, even for a beggar who may ask a penny of him. If he does not have a penny to give, let him politely say to the beggar that his circumstances or obligations are such that he cannot grant the favor, expressing sympathy for the unfortunate, if he thinks he is worthy of it. (1899)

In the Depot

1889

Should all the seats in the depot be occupied, let the men always give up theirs to the woman who may not be seated and let the younger men give theirs to the aged and feeble men. (1899)

Women on a Train

Women, in particular, should remember that they have not chartered the whole car, but only paid for a small fraction of it, and be careful not to monopolize the dressing room for two or three hours at a stretch, while half a dozen or more fellow-travelers are waiting outside to arrange their toilets. (1910)

Sleeping Berths

When you intend to take a sleeping berth, secure your ticket for it a day or two before you intend starting, so as to obtain a desirable location. A lower berth in the center of the car is always the most comfortable, as you escape the jar of the wheels and the opening door. (1910)

1897

1912

Fashion on a Train

A lady will avoid overdressing in traveling. Silks and velvets, laces and jewelry are completely out of place on a railway train. Some women have the idea that any old thing is good enough to travel in, and so look exceedingly shabby on the train. This is a mistake. (1910)

Healthy Young Women

No women who is young and well should feel aggrieved if a man keeps his seat while she has none. (1910)

Rush Hour

Those wishing to board a train should patiently wait until all the passengers who are leaving the train have got off; for if they rush upon the steps or platform or into the aisle of the coach, they will likely so jam the passageway as to make it difficult for them to pass in and others to pass out. All should avoid rushing to get in advance of others. (1899)

> *"If any passenger be guilty of disorderly conduct or breach of the peace, or use any obscene, profane, or vulgar language, of playing any game of cards or other games of chance for money or other thing of value, or of selling or of offering for sale a lottery ticket upon any passenger train, the conductor of the train may stop it at the place where the offense is committed, or at the next stopping place of the train, and eject such passenger from the train, using only such force as may be necessary to accomplish the removal.* **(Mississippi Code Section 3563, 1899)**

Silence is Golden

No one should sing, whistle, or talk loud or laugh immoderately in the sitting room or in the depot at all. (1899)

1880

Travel by Rail

1878

Folks, Please Be Calm

It is not polite to rush for the best seats, nor to occupy more room than you are fairly entitled to. In steam railway carriages you pay for one seat — do not claim two. Do not talk or laugh in such a manner as to attract public attention. (1900)

Hat Etiquette

On a railroad a man removes his hat in a parlor-car, but not in a day coach. (1904)

Ladies Come First

If women apply at the door, when you are occupying the best seat in the coach, you must give place to them. (1836)

1879

Old Lady: "I should like a ticket for the train." Ticket Clerk, who thinks he will make a joke: "Yes madam. Will you go in the passenger train, or in the cattle train" Old Lady: "Well, if you are a specimen of what I shall find in the passenger train, give me a ticket for the cattle train, by all means." (Frank Leslie's Pleasant Hours, 1885)

Trying to eat a 30 cent lunch in a nickel's worth of time. —

1912

Intemperance

Politeness allows no drinking of whiskey, wine, or any other intemperate drink, much less drunkenness, on the train. A person who would do such a thing is void of common self-respect, much less true politeness. It is quite offensive and sickening to have to smell the breath of a whiskey drinker anywhere, and how much more so when shut up with him in a passenger coach! (1899)

Window Etiquette

Passengers should not hoist and keep hoisted a window in the winter, to the damage and discomfort of others. Some who travel have poor health, and their condition is such that a current of cold air on them a short while increases their trouble and endangers their lives. A person may be in very good health and yet be made sick in a few minutes by a cold draught. (1899)

Avoid a Hack

In arriving at a station in a large city where she is a stranger, a lady should avoid taking a hack, choose instead horse-cars, or the stages plying between stations. (1889)

The Railway Janitor

The janitor should not whistle, sing or indulge blustering speech in the sitting room, nor make himself unpleasant to the passengers in any respect. (1899)

Traveling with Diamonds

O N the steamboat, or on the stagecoach, surely camel's-hair and diamonds are out of place; yet one very representative political lady defended her fine clothes by saying she "always wore them traveling, to show them." (1884b)

1899

Don't be a Glutton

In steamers do not make a rush for the supper table, or make a glutton of yourself when you get there. (1881)

Flirting on a Steamboat

The practice of some young girls just entering into womanhood, of flirting with any young man they may chance to meet, either in a railway car or on a steamboat, indicates low-breeding in the extreme. If, however, the journey is long, and especially if it be on a steamboat, a certain sociability may be allowed, and a married lady or a lady of middle age may use her privileges to make the journey an enjoyable one, for fellow-passengers should always be sociable to one another. (1882)

Discretion in Forming Acquaintances

While an acquaintance formed in a railway car or on a steamboat, continues only during the trip, discretion should be used in making acquaintances. Ladies may, as has been stated, accept small courtesies and favors from strangers, but must check at once any attempt at familiarity. On the other hand, no man who pretends to be a gentleman will attempt any familiarity. (1882)

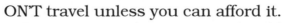

DON'T travel unless you can afford it.

• Don't carry a chip on your shoulder. Most people you meet are well-disposed and kind.

• Don't permit your children, if you have any with you, to annoy people with ill-bred behavior.

• Don't exchange visiting cards with strangers, unless this is justified by exceptional circumstances.

• Don't return civility with the opposite.

• Don't fail to assist any infirm, crippled, or aged fellow-traveler if they need a helping hand.

• Don't, by a single thought or action, add to the burden of the sorrow now pressing so heavily upon many fellow-pilgrims.

• Don't forget that most of the evil passions are traceable to two roots, anger and worry. These are the thieves that steal precious time and energy from your life. Anger is a highway robber; and worry is a sneak thief.

• Do not fan so vigorously that a cold current chills the back of your neighbor's neck.

1889

• Do not tread on people's feet.

• Never engage in altercations with bumptious people who wish to pick a quarrel.

• When escorting ladies be polite but not belligerent. It is most embarrassing to a woman to be the subject of a quarrel, as to a seat, or somebody's cigar, or any other passing annoyance. (1910)

Expectoration

For the hygiene and comfort of travelers, the revolting habit of expectoration in public conveyances is a thing of the past; prohibited under penalties of fine and imprisonment by modern boards of health, it has had its odious day, and no longer moves fastidious strangers from abroad to write of us as if we were a hoard of barbarians instead of a refined and wholesome nation,

1880

with standards of purity and excellence to maintain. (1910)

Agreeable Travelers

The most polite, as well as agreeable travellers are those who will smilingly devour mouse-pie and bird's-nest soup in China, dine contentedly upon horse-steak in Paris, swallow their beef uncooked in Germany, maintain an unwinking gravity over the hottest curry in India, smoke their hookah gratefully in Turkey, mount an elephant in Ceylon, and, in short, conform gracefully to any native custom, however strange it may appear to him. (1869)

1901

Shabby Clothes

In preparing for a journey, you should put on the shabbiest clothes you have, provided they are consistent with decency; none but very vulgar persons wear their best coat in a stage-coach. You should have a coloured cravat, a dark waistcoat, and a cap. (1836)

Clothes Make the Man

OWEVER ugly you may be, rest assured that there is some style of habiliment which will make you passable. (1836)

Making a Spectacle Out of Yourself

If you have bad, squinting eyes, which have lost their lashes and are bordered with red, you should wear spectacles. If the defect is great, your glasses should be coloured. (1836)

Ugly Enough

It is evident, therefore, that although a man may be ugly, there is no necessity for his being shocking. (1836)

Become a Hermit

If you have any defect, so shocking and so ridiculous as to procure you a nickname, then indeed there is but one remedy — to renounce society. (1836)

Umbrella Etiquette

MBRELLAS are an instrument of peace rather than a weapon of war. (1896)

If carrying an umbrella, avoid striking it against those who pass you. If you are walking with a lady, let the umbrella cover her perfectly, but hold it so you do not touch her bonnet. (1875)

1883

Do not carry an umbrella laterally under your arm. It may poke someone's eyes out. (1910)

No gentleman swings his stick or umbrella about when walking, as he would be in danger of bestowing a gratuitous and unexpected blow on a passer-by, who might make him rue his carelessness and rudeness. (1885)

Etiquette Quiz
Should a lady accept an umbrella offered by a strange gentleman?

No, such an offer must be firmly, yet politely, declined. (1892)

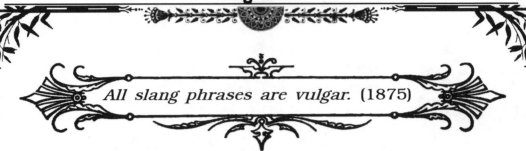

All slang phrases are vulgar. (1875)

Vulgar Acts

When committed in the presence of others the following acts are classed as vulgarities.

- To stand or sit with feet wide apart.
- To hum, whistle, or sing in suppressed tones.
- To use profane language, or stronger expression than the occasion justifies.
- To chew tobacco, and its necessary accompaniment, spitting, are vulgar in the extreme.
- To correct inaccuracies in the speech of others, or in the mode of their speech.
- To stand with arms a-kimbo; or to lounge or yawn, or do anything which shows disrespect, selfishness or indifference. (1893)

Such exclamations as "The Dickens," or "Mercy," or "Good Gracious," should never be used. If you are surprised or astonished, suppress the fact. Such expressions border closely on profanity. (1889b)

There is no surer sign of vulgarity than the perpetual boasting of the fine things you have at home — If you speak of your silver, of your jewelry, of your costly apparel, it will be taken for a sign that you are either lying, or that you were, not long ago, somebody's washerwoman, and cannot forget to be reminding everybody that you are not so now. (1860)

There cannot be a custom more vulgar or offensive than that of taking a person aside to whisper, in a room with company; yet this rudeness is of too frequent occurrence. (1838)

Kissing the Bride

HE practice of kissing the bride is not so common as formerly. (1864)

Unkissed Lips

If young people would meet each other at the marriage altar with unkissed lips, there would be few blighted lives and wrecked homes. (1916)

Bridal Carriage

Carriages should be provided to take the bride and her family to the church and back to the house, and also the guests from the church to the receptions. The expense is borne by the family of the bride, save for the carriage used by the groom, which takes him and the best man to the church, and later takes the married couple to the house, and after the reception, to the station. (1904)

Dancing at the Wedding

A bride does not usually dance at her own wedding, but she may join in a square dance if she chooses. (1887)

Etiquette Quiz

Is it "good form," to kiss the bride at the close of the marriage ceremony?

The custom is almost obsolete. (1889)

Old Shoes

As the couple pass out of the front door it is customary for the guests to throw after them, for luck, rice, rose leaves, flowers, old shoes, etc. (1904)

Wedding Fees

The wedding fee, preferably gold or clean bills in sealed envelope, is given by the best man to the officiating clergyman. Custom leaves the amount to the groom, who should give at least five dollars or more, in proportion to his income and social position. The clergyman usually gives the fee to his wife. (1904)

Duties of a Wife

IT is upon the wife that the happiness of home chiefly depends. It is her privilege and pleasure to promote domestic felicity and garland her husband's house with the flowers of a sweet and helpful life. (1892)

1909

Practice Economy

The young wife can not be too careful in her expenditures. "My husband works hard for every dollar he earns and it seems to me worse than cruel to lay out a dime unnecessarily." (1892)

Avoid Bickering

Painstakingly avoid all bickerings. A small concession will often prevent a serious misunderstanding. In the woman who is married to a man disposed to irascibility the wisest discretion is demanded. If she fails to command her own temper, that of her husband is certain to be tried and bitter heart-burnings will follow. (1892)

Moral Pruning-Knife

A wife is the grand wielder of the moral pruning-knife. (1894)

Mind Your Temper

She should never indulge in fits of temper, hysterics, or other habits of ill-breeding, which, though easy to conquer at first, grow and strengthen with indulgence. (1882)

Beware of Confidants

Beware of intrusting any individual whatever with small annoyances, or misunderstandings, between your husband and yourself, if they unhappily occur. Confidants are dangerous persons, and many seek to obtain an ascendancy in families by gaining the good opinion of young married women. Be on your guard, and reject every overture that may lead to undesirable intimacy. Should any one presume to offer you advice with regard to your husband, or seek to lessen him by insinuations, shun that person as you would a serpent. (1881)

1882

Neat and Tidy

She should be equally as neat and tidy respecting her dress and personal appearance at home as when she appears in society, and her manners towards her husband should be as kind and pleasing when alone with him as when in company. (1882)

High and Lofty Thoughts

She should lead her husband to high and noble thoughts, lofty aims, and temporal comfort; be ever ready to welcome him home. (1882)

1903

Woman Suffrage

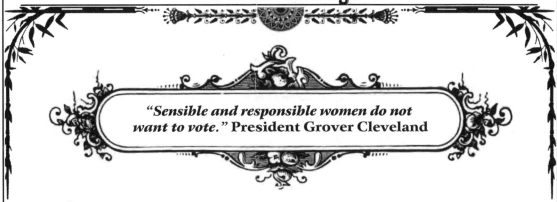

"Sensible and responsible women do not want to vote." President Grover Cleveland

Fervor and Fury

large part of the suffrage movement at present, in its fervor and fury, represents the acme of hysterical feminine thoughtlessness and unrest. (1913)

Limited Suffrage

It must be remembered that twenty-six states in the Union have today some form of limited female suffrage, which, however, is of so little interest to the women concerned that the voting right is very rarely used. It is estimated that less than 2 per cent of the New England women who are entitled and urged to vote upon school matters, ever take advantage of their opportunity. (1913)

Shall women vote? No, they might disturb the existing order of things. (*Puck Magazine*, 1909)

1909

> *If women are given the ballot, it will bear very heavily upon her.* (1913)

Exhaustion of The Vital Force

Women are everywhere today suffering from exhaustion of vital force, due to the incessant demands of a life crowded with claims outside the home, either in social obligations, philanthropic or civic interests, or the taxing strain of industrial life. Between these two comes the large percentage of American women, far larger than any other class, who need all their strength for necessary household tasks. (1913)

An Irreparable Calamity

It will be an irreparable calamity to extend further the suffrage to woman. It is important that woman should be aware of that fact, and equally so that man should see clearly how to vindicate himself from the charge of oppression and tyranny. (1909b)

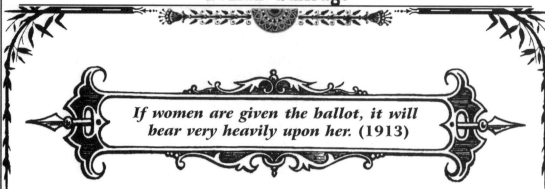

JUSTICE TO WOMEN

Susan B. Anthony 1820–1906
Pioneer Worker for Woman Suffrage

She spoke before every Congress from 1869 to 1906.

"Let every woman who enjoys the freedom she helped to win and every man who rejoices in the larger horizon of the mothers of his race, give loving homage to the great heart and dauntless spirit of Susan B. Anthony."

MAKERS OF AMERICAN IDEALS

1909

> *The ballot is not a right denied; it is a burden removed.* (1913)

Woman Suffrage

The Limit of Nerve-Tax

In the carrying out of political plans, a woman will be at the mercy of her nature. For one whole year, if a new life is to emerge, she is unfit to assume additional risk in the overstrain of her normally taxed nervous system. Maternity is an exhibition of a woman's nervous system taxed to a normal limit, and normally entirely equal to the strain. But while pregnancy is not a pathological condition, it is the limit of nerve-tax. Presumably there are other children and a home. How much more ought a woman to do? (1913)

Temperamental Disabilities

There is also a temperamental difference in men and women which makes an equal footing in political life all but impossible. Whatever she may have had in the past, whatever she may be going to have in the future, at the present moment she has great temperamental disabilities. (1913)

Nervous Stability

The average woman has as much brains as the average man, and average persons are going to do the greater part of the voting, but the woman lacks endurance in things mental; her fortitudes are physical and spiritual. She lacks nervous stability. The suffragists who dismay England are nerve-sick women. (1913)

1909

What Will Happen When the Polling Place is Located in a Millenary Shop?

Exercising the Franchise

A lady, advocating woman suffrage, recently made the following argument: "I have no vote, but my groom has. I have a great respect for that man in the stables; but I am sure, if I were to go to him and say, "John, will you exercise the franchise?" he would reply, "Please, ma'am, which horse be that?" (*Frank Leslie's Pleasant Hours*, 1885)

A Menace to Womanhood

We of the majority insist that universal adult suffrage will be a menace to American government and to American womanhood, and that it is lacking in the fundamental principle of patriotism. (1913)

A Terrible Strain on the Family

Suffrage will place a new and terrible strain upon the family relation. (1909b)

THE STEAM ROLLER
1909

Woman Suffrage

Rash Ventures

America is a vigorous young leader in the family of nations. It should not have its progress checked by rash ventures which have to do with the very foundations of its governmental life. (1913)

Suffering No Wrongs

We submit the proposition that American women, judged not by the individual, the group, or the class, but as a whole, are suffering under no wrongs which need for their redress the violent overturning of the entire political machinery of the nation. (1913)

Giddap
1914

Library of Congress

1917

Let Well Enough Alone

Instead of embracing the cause of Suffrage let us have the fortitude to resist and to reject emphatically and cast out this modern heresy, and so keep out of the political quagmire we would surely fall into if we ever adopted this false doctrine. (1913b)

1915

Misery and Disaster

The Suffragette is a movement which may entail more misery and disaster on the human race than any of the scourges which have yet afflicted it. (1913b)

Domestic Anarchy

What all the resulting evils would be, each man can try to imagine for himself, but it seems that among them there would surely be domestic anarchy, loss of all power and influence in the family on the part of husbands and fathers, more severe forms of

1915

slavery for them, more divorces, ruinous decrees for alimony, the prison, work in chains on the public roads, neglect, despair, murder, and suicide. All these calamities can be counted upon to appear like so many specters in the dark when the sun of man's political power shall have set. (1913b)

1914

"Woman: queen of the cookstove throne." (1914)

Character and Penmanship

HARACTER is frequently judged by handwriting. Write a good, clear, legible hand, without any flourishes, and always use the best and the blackest of ink. The typewriter is employed only for business correspondence. For social correspondence use only Irish-linen white note paper unruled, with square envelopes to match. Fancy or tinted note paper of any kind is vulgar. (1896)

Writing a Good Hand

To write a good hand is an essential accomplishment which every woman should acquire. (*The Ladies' World*, June, 1897)

Refinement in Writing

Plain white unruled paper is always the most refined and elegant for note-paper and envelopes, though a delicate gray is not in bad taste. Place the postage stamp in a straight, that is, vertical position, in the upper right hand of the envelope. It argues great carelessness to put the stamp on in any sort of a fashion. (*The Ladies' World*, June, 1897)

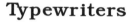

Typewriters

What we should do without the little machine that serves us so faithfully I do not know. The typewriter is limited to business purposes. It cannot be used for personal letters, love-letters, or letters of an intimate, personal, or confidential character. (1910)

1900

The first requisites for letters are pens, ink and paper.

Very Bad Penmanship

The boy who would pick up the half consumed cigar and smoke out the balance of the stump, thinking that thereby he makes a man of himself, will look upon bad penmanship, when executed by distinguished men, as an evidence of genius, and is not unlikely to imagine himself a great man, because he imitates their pot-hooks and scrawls. (1883)

Fun at Home

HOMES are often are deserts of monotony. A little fun is the very best preventive against bad manners that can be imagined. Why not have games in the evening or music? In some houses, the father dozes on the lounge all the evening. The boys skip out of the house the moment supper is over. You see no more of them till a late bedtime. By and by they form undesirable associations — get into bad company, start on the downhill road. It is not too much to say that fun at ome would have saved many a lad from ruin. (1910)

1912

The thoughtlessness, selfishness, and rudeness of too many young men and women attest the folly of supposing that true good manners will form themselves. (1887)

Don't Be Sarcastic

DEAR girls, if you want to be popular, or if you want to have sincere friends, never indulge in sarcasm, for there is nothing loveable or attractive about a sarcastic woman. She never has any friends but policy friends. The sarcastic habit grows upon a person very rapidly, so if you are just a little sarcastic as girls, you will some day, if you live, become sarcastic old women. Who loves or admires

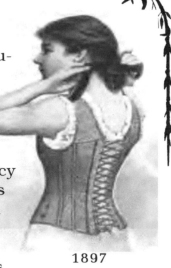

1897

the disagreeable old person, who with her arrows of sarcasm wounds the hearts of all those with whom she comes in contact? (*The Ladies' World*, June, 1897)

A growing girl should not wear a corset. **(1910)**

The Snares of Cupid

If you have a wholesome dread of being entangled, and watch over your preferences with a jealous eye, you need never be caught in the snares of Cupid. (1838)

Rude Play

Never join in rude play, as this will subject you to being kissed or handled by gentlemen. Do not suffer your hand to be held or squeezed, but showing that it displeases you by instantly withdrawing it. Be not lifted in or out of carriages, or on or off a horse. (1838)

1880

1892

The Opposite Sex

Women are happily endowed with a quick sense of propriety, and a natural modesty, which will generally guide them aright in their intercourse with the other sex, and the more perfectly well-bred and discreet you are, in your intercourse with female friends, the more easy will it be for you to acquit yourself well with your male ones. (1838)

The less your mind dwells upon lovers and matrimony, the more agreeable and profitable will be your intercourse with gentlemen. (1838)

The Lure of Kissing

Girls, it is in bad taste for you to be given to kissing boys or men...a kiss is nothing more or less than a physical sounding of a woman's social, mental, or moral strength. (1889)

Young girls should wear white as much as possible. It is not proper for you to receive calls from young men, and it is extremely improper to allow them to kiss you. (*The Peoples Home Journal,* January, 1907)

You Must Wait!

Never condescend to use little arts and maneuvers, to secure a pleasant beau at a party or an excursion; remember that a woman must always wait to be chosen. (1838)

1900

Advantages of Rising Early

Industry is up with the sun; she awaketh with the crowing of the cock; and walketh abroad to taste the sweetness of the morning. Her garment sweepeth the dewdrop from the new stubble and the green grass, and her path is by the murmuring of the purling brook. Her appetite is keen; her blood is pure and temperate and her pulse beateth even. Her house is elegant, her handmaids are the daughters of neatness, and plenty smileth at her table. She saunters not, neither stretcheth herself out on the couch of indolence. (1838)

The Evils of Rising Late

Her body is enfeebled, and her eyes are heavy; her mind is stupefied, her devotions are neglected, or hastily performed; her toilet is slovenly and incomplete, her morning meal is taken alone, or with those who are annoyed at having waited for her; and the attendants are out of humor. To all this may be added a painful sense of ill desert hanging like a mill-stone round her neck all day. (1838)

1903

"For good times, for romance, for society, college life offers unequaled opportunities."
Wellesley College girl, 1890s

Microbes by the Hundred

One shudders to think of the pollution gathered up by a skirt that not merely touches but drags on the sidewalk, gathering up microbes by the hundred, and bringing into a clean house dirt of every description. (1910)

Mistrust a flatterer. (1838)

The Duty of Girls

It is not enough that a young lady should sing and play and dance well; she should be able likewise to sew and cook well. She should know how to darn a stocking as well as how to paint a panel. And she should not forget that there is quite as fine (and perhaps a nobler) art in baking a loaf of good bread or making a cake as there is in rendering a Beethoven sonata. (1892)

Your Parents' Approval

A good guide to your conduct is to ask yourself whether you are willing to have your father and mother know what you are doing. You will make few mistakes in doing only what you know they approve. (*The People's Home Journal*, June, 1907)

Associating with a Libertine

Do not be afraid to refuse the acquaintance of a known libertine, it is a tribute which you owe to virtue, and, if generally paid, would do more to purify society, and to keep the moral standards of it high, than the laws of the land or the eloquence of the pulpit. (1838)

A Head Full of Nonsense

Lively, ingenious, conversable and charming little girls, often spoil into dull, bashful, silent young ladies, all because their heads are full of nonsense about beaux and lovers. (1838)

Bibliography

1836 - Laws of Etiquette, or Short Rules and Reflections For Conduct in Society by a Gentleman.

1838 - The Young Lady's Friend by Mrs. John Farrar.

1841 - Gentleman and Lady's Book of Politeness by Elisabeth Celnart.

1843 - Hints on Etiquette and the Usages of Society by Charles William Day.

1846 - The Book of Snobs by William Makepeace Thackeray.

1859 - Beatle's Dime Book of Etiquette by A Committee of Three.

1859b-The Moral Philosophy of Courtship and Marriage by William A. Abbott, MD.

1860 - The Perfect Gentleman by A Gentleman.

1864 - How to Do It by John Tingley.

1868 - Manners by Sarah Josepha Buell Hale.

1869 - Frost's Laws & By-laws of American Society.

1875 - Gentleman's Book of Etiquette and Manual of Politeness by Cecil B. Hartley.

1880 - Home and Health and Home Economics by C. H. Fowler.

1881 - Decorum: A Practical Treatise on Etiquette and Dress of the Best American by John A. Ruth.

1882 - Our Deportment by John H. Young.

1883 - Hill's Manual of Social and Business Forms by Thomas Edie Hill.

1884 - Don't by Oliver Bell Bunce.

1884b-Etiquette, the American Code of Manners by Mrs. M. E. W. Sherwood.

1885 - Etiquette by Lady Constance Howard.

1886 - How to be Happy Though Married by a Graduate in the University of Matrimony.

1887 - Social Customs by Florence Howe Hall.

1888 - How To Teach Manners by Mrs. Julia M. Dewey.

1889 - The Home Manual by John A. Logan.

1889b-Polite Life and Etiquette by Walter Houghton.

1889c-Elementary Psychology by Daniel Putnam.

1889d-Good Manners by Eliza M. Lavin.

1892 - Our Manners and Social Customs by Daphne Dale.

Bibliography

1892b-Poems and Prose by John Christie.

1893 - Rules of Etiquette and Home Culture by Walter Houghton

1893b-Etiquette by Agnes H. Morton.

1894 - Manners, Culture and Dress of the Best American Society by Richard A. Wells.

1894b-Right Living by Susan H. Wixon.

1896 - The Complete Bachelor by Walter Germain.

1896b-Social Etiquette by Maud C. Cooke.

1896c-The House and Home by Dr. Lyman Abbott, et. al.

1897 - Manners For Men by Mrs. Humphry.

1899 - Politeness on Railroads by Isaac L. Peebles.

1899b-Lessons on Morals by Julia M. Dewey.

1900 - A Primer of Ethics by Benjamin B. Comegys.

1901 - The Spinster Book by Myrtle Rood.

1902 - The Strenuous Life by Theodore Roosevelt.

1904 - A Dictionary of Etiquette by Walter Cox Green.

1905 - Everyday Etiquette, a Manual on Social Uses by Marion Hartland and Virginia Van De Water.

1905b-Boys and Their Management in School by H. Bompas Smith.

1906 - The Happy Motorist by Filson Young.

1906b-Eediotic Etiquette by Gideon Wurdz.

1907 - The Blue Book of Etiquette For Women by Mrs. Charles Harcourt.

1908 - Manners for the Metropolis by Frank Crowninshield.

1909 - The Woman and the Car by Dorothy Levitt.

1909b-The Wrong & Peril of Woman Suffrage by James Buckley.

1909c-A Handbook of Hospitality for Town and Country by Florence Howe Hall.

1910 - Good Manners for All Occasions by Margaret Elizabeth Munson Sangster.

1910b-The Bolster Book by Harry Graham,

1912 - Manners and Social Usages by Arthur M. Sherwood.

1913 - Anti-Suffrage: Ten Good Reasons by Grace Goodwin.

1913b-Shall Women Vote? A Book For Men by Conway Sams.

1916 - Eugenics by T.W. Shannon.